*~ All Time ~*

# FAMILY FAVORITES™

# BREAKFAST & BRUNCH

PUBLICATIONS INTERNATIONAL, LTD.

Front cover photography by Burke/Triolo Productions, Culver City, CA

**Pictured on the front cover:** Blueberry-Cheese Pancakes *(page 60)*.
**Pictured on the back cover:** French Raisin Toast *(page 58)*.

ISBN: 0-7853-1194-7

Manufactured in U.S.A.

8 7 6 5 4 3 2 1

**Microwave Cooking:** Microwave ovens may vary in wattage. The microwave cooking times given in this publication are approximate. Use the cooking times as guidelines and check for doneness before adding more time. Consult manufacturer's instructions for suitable microwave-safe dishes.

# — Contents —

# — Rise 'n' Shine —

The first meal of the day can be a delightful as well as delicious passage from dreamland to reality. Even if you are still half asleep until after that first cup of coffee, you'll appreciate this fantastic collection of easy-to-make breakfast and brunch recipes. Morning is a wonderful time to entertain family and friends. People are hungry, relaxed and refreshed after a good night's sleep and are appreciative of a delicious morning meal.

If you're a "no time for breakfast" person, check out the *Zippy Breakfasts in a Flash* chapter. It contains many great ideas for super-fast breakfasts—many which are perfect for eating on the run! When you are in the mood for a more leisurely meal, be sure to read the chapter called *Elegant Brunch Dishes*. It is full of exceptional dishes that will satisfy even the heartiest appetites. To round out your meal, there are chapters on *Sunny Breakfast Basics*, *Glorious Egg Entrées* and *Dazzling Breads & Coffee Cakes*. And through each chapter you'll find brand name recipes from your favorite companies.

Before you begin planning your next breakfast or brunch, take some time to read through these guidelines. You'll find hints on choosing and preparing all kinds of breakfast and brunch fare.

## BEVERAGES

**Juices:** Dress up juices or juice-blends by serving them in a fancy goblet or champagne flute. Add pieces of frozen fruit (grapes and berries work particularly well) or freeze mint leaves or lemon peel in ice cubes.

**Coffee:** Coffee lovers swear by a steaming cup of good coffee as a important part of breakfast. It's easy to make a perfect cup of coffee by following these tips: Freshness is one key to great coffee; either grind the beans yourself or keep ground coffee in the freezer. Use the grind recommended for your type of coffeemaker. For a good medium-strength cup of coffee, use about 2 tablespoons of coffee for each cup to be made. Vary this amount to suit your taste. Be sure the coffeemaker is clean and thoroughly rinsed. Use the correct amount of freshly drawn cold water and follow the manufacturer's directions for brewing. *Never allow coffee to boil;* high heat will ruin even the best coffee flavor.

**Tea:** Many people prefer a cup of fragrant tea as their breakfast beverage. Tea bags are the easiest way to make tea. Pour boiling water on top of a tea bag in a cup. Let it steep 2 to 5 minutes (the longer it steeps, the stronger the flavor). Remove the tea bag before drinking. To make larger quantities, use a teapot. Warm the teapot first by swirling it with very hot water. Place 1 teaspoon loose tea for each serving plus 1 extra teaspoon into the teapot (or use a tea ball). Pour boiling water (1 cup for each serving) over the tea and let it steep 3 to 6 minutes. Strain the tea into cups and enjoy.

## EGGS

Eggs can be prepared in a great variety of ways, many of which you'll see in this publication. Eggs are best when cooked over low to medium heat and stirred as little as possible. If overcooked, they become dry and tough, so be gentle and your eggs will be a taste treat. For safety reasons always use clean, uncracked grade A eggs and cook them until the yolks are thickened and set.

## BREAKFAST MEATS

**Bacon:** Crisp-cooked bacon is a wonderful accompaniment to all kinds of breakfast and brunch foods. Bacon is highly perishable and should be used soon after purchasing. It will keep in the refrigerator about 10 days or can be frozen for up to 3 months. Bacon can be cooked in a skillet over medium-high heat, baked on a rack in a baking pan at 350°F or cooked in the microwave layered between paper towels on a microwave-safe

rack at HIGH (100%). Whatever the method, always be extremely careful—bacon grease gets very hot!

**Canadian Bacon:** More like ham than bacon, this lean smoked meat is a popular breakfast food. Because it is purchased fully cooked, it heats quickly in a skillet over medium-high heat.

**Sausage:** Sausage is available in a variety of shapes and flavorings and may be fresh, partially cooked, smoked or fully cooked. The method for cooking varies with the type of sausage used. Cook all fresh sausage until it is no longer pink in the center and is heated through.

## FRUITS

Fruits can add color and elegance to any breakfast or brunch spread. They provide many nutrients and as an attention-getter, you can't beat the appeal of a big bowl of fresh cut-up fruit.

Use fruit as a garnish to brighten up an appetizer tray, a frittata dish or a bread basket. Strawberries, blackberries, raspberries and grape clusters make excellent eye-catching additions to any plate. Remember, most fruits are jam-packed with vitamins, such as C and A, and fiber. What a great way to start your day!

*— Sunny —*

# BREAKFAST BASICS

## THREE-EGG OMELET

**1 tablespoon butter or margarine**
**3 eggs, lightly beaten**
    **Salt and freshly ground pepper to taste**
    **Fillings (see below)**

**1**. Melt butter in 10-inch skillet over medium heat.

**2**. Add eggs; lift cooked edges with spatula to allow uncooked eggs to flow under cooked portion. Season with salt and pepper. Shake pan to loosen omelet. Cook until set. Place desired fillings on ½ of omelet. Fold in half. Turn out onto plate.

*Makes 1 serving*

---

### *Filling Suggestions*

| | |
|---|---|
| *Shredded cheese* | *Cooked small shrimp* |
| *Shredded crabmeat* | *Cooked chopped* |
| *Cooked sliced* | *  bell pepper* |
| *  mushrooms* | *Chopped tomatoes* |
| *Cooked chopped onion* | *Cooked chopped* |
| *Avocado slices* | *  asparagus or broccoli* |
| *Chopped ham* | |

# BREAKFAST BASICS

## STRAWBERRY SAUCE

**1 pint strawberries, hulled**
**2 to 3 tablespoons sugar**
**1 tablespoon strawberry- or orange-flavored**
**liqueur (optional)**

Combine strawberries, sugar and liqueur in blender or food processor. Cover; process until strawberries are puréed. *Makes 1½ cups*

## HOT CHOCOLATE

**3 ounces semisweet chocolate, finely**
**chopped**
**¼ to ½ cup sugar**
**4 cups milk, divided**
**1 teaspoon vanilla extract**
**Whipped cream or marshmallows**
**(optional)**

**1.** Combine chocolate, sugar and ¼ cup milk in medium saucepan over medium-low heat. Cook, stirring constantly, until chocolate melts. Add remaining 3¾ cups milk; heat until hot, stirring occasionally. *Do not boil.* Stir in vanilla.

**2.** Beat with whisk until frothy. Pour into mugs and top with whipped cream or marshmallows, if desired. *Makes 4 servings*

**HOT COCOA:** Substitute ¼ cup unsweetened cocoa powder for semisweet chocolate and use ½ cup sugar; heat as above.

**HOT MOCHA:** Add 4 teaspoons instant coffee to milk mixture; heat as above.

## WAFFLES

**2¼ cups all-purpose flour**
**2 tablespoons sugar**
**1 tablespoon baking powder**
**½ teaspoon salt**
**2 eggs, beaten**
**¼ cup vegetable oil**
**2 cups milk**
**Strawberry Sauce (see recipe this page)**

**1.** Preheat waffle iron; grease lightly.

**2.** Sift flour, sugar, baking powder and salt into large bowl. Combine eggs, oil and milk in medium bowl. Stir liquid ingredients into dry ingredients until moistened.

**3.** For each waffle, pour about ¾ cup of batter into waffle iron. Close lid and bake until steaming stops.* Serve with Strawberry Sauce.
*Makes about 6 round waffles*

*Check the manufacturer's directions for recommended amount of batter and baking time.

> *For crispier waffles, use less batter and let them cook for a few seconds longer after the steaming has stopped.*

*Waffle with Strawberry Sauce*

# BREAKFAST BASICS

## GARLIC SKILLET POTATOES

   2 tablespoons vegetable or olive oil
   4 large red-skinned potatoes, cut into thin
      wedges
 ½ cup chopped onion
1¼ teaspoons LAWRY'S® Garlic Powder with
      Parsley
 ¾ to 1 teaspoon LAWRY'S® Seasoned Salt
 ¾ teaspoon LAWRY'S® Seasoned Pepper
 ½ teaspoon sugar
   Chopped fresh parsley (garnish)

In large skillet, heat oil over medium heat. Add potatoes, onion, Garlic Powder with Parsley, Seasoned Salt, Seasoned Pepper and sugar. Cook, uncovered, over medium heat 25 to 30 minutes or until potatoes are tender and browned.

*Makes 4 to 6 servings*

**PRESENTATION:** Sprinkle with chopped parsley. Great served with scrambled eggs or omelets.

## BERRY CRÊPES WITH ORANGE SAUCE

   1 cup fresh blueberries
   1 cup sliced strawberries
   1 tablespoon sugar
   3 packages (3 ounces each) cream cheese,
      softened
 ¼ cup honey
 ¾ cup orange juice
   8 (6½-inch) Crêpes (page 24)

**1.** Combine blueberries, strawberries and sugar in small bowl; set aside.

**2.** To prepare sauce, beat cream cheese and honey until light; slowly beat in orange juice.

**3.** Spoon about ½ cup of berry filling in center of 1 crêpe. Spoon about 1 tablespoon sauce over berries. Roll up; place on serving plate. Repeat with remaining crêpes.

**4.** Pour remaining sauce over crêpes.

*Makes 4 servings*

*Garlic Skillet Potatoes*

## BREAKFAST BASICS

## BUTTERMILK PANCAKES

2 cups all-purpose flour
1 tablespoon sugar
1½ teaspoons baking powder
½ teaspoon baking soda
½ teaspoon salt
1 egg, beaten
1½ cups buttermilk
¼ cup vegetable oil

**1.** Sift flour, sugar, baking powder, baking soda and salt into large bowl.

**2.** Combine egg, buttermilk and oil in medium bowl. Stir liquid ingredients into dry ingredients until moistened.

**3.** Preheat griddle or large skillet over medium heat; grease lightly. Pour about ½ cup batter onto hot griddle for each pancake. Cook until tops of pancakes are bubbly and appear dry; turn and cook until browned, about 2 minutes.

*Makes about 12 (5-inch) pancakes*

**SILVER DOLLAR PANCAKES:** Use 1 tablespoon batter for each pancake. Cook as above. Makes about 40 pancakes.

---

### *Buttermilk Substitution*

*If you don't have buttermilk on hand,
try this easy substitution:*

*Place 1 tablespoon vinegar in measuring cup.
Add milk to measure 1½ cups.
Stir well; let stand 5 minutes.*

---

## DATE-NUT GRANOLA

2 cups rolled oats
2 cups barley flakes
1 cup sliced almonds
⅓ cup vegetable oil
⅓ cup honey
1 teaspoon vanilla extract
1 cup chopped dates

**1.** Preheat oven to 350°F. Grease 13×9-inch baking pan.

**2.** Combine oats, barley flakes and almonds in large bowl; set aside.

**3.** Combine oil, honey and vanilla in small bowl. Pour honey mixture over oat mixture; stir well. Pour into prepared pan.

**4.** Bake about 25 minutes or until toasted, stirring frequently after the first 10 minutes. Stir in dates while mixture is still hot. Cool. Store tightly covered.

*Makes 6 cups*

***Top to bottom:*** *Summer Berries* (page 15)
*and Date-Nut Granola*

## BREAKFAST BASICS

## SCRAMBLED EGGS

**1 tablespoon butter or margarine**
**6 eggs, lightly beaten**
**½ teaspoon salt**
**¼ teaspoon freshly ground pepper**

**1.** Melt butter in 10-inch skillet over medium heat.

**2.** Season eggs with salt and pepper. Add eggs to skillet; cook, stirring gently and lifting to allow uncooked eggs to flow under cooked portion. Do not overcook; eggs should be soft with no liquid remaining. *Makes 4 servings*

---

*Scrambled Egg Options*

*Add one or more of the following to the beaten egg mixture and cook as above:*

*Chopped fresh herbs*
*Diced green chilies*
*Cooked chopped onions*
*Chopped sun-dried tomatoes*
*Cooked chopped vegetables*
*Shredded cheese*
*Crumbled cooked bacon or cooked sausage*
*Chopped smoked salmon*
*Chopped ham or Canadian bacon*

---

## HASH-STUFFED POTATOES

**4 large baking potatoes (10 to 12 ounces each)**
**1 can (15 ounces) corned beef hash**
**4 eggs**

**1.** Preheat oven to 350°F.

**2.** Cut thin slice from top of each potato. Using melon baller, scoop out insides of each potato, leaving a ½-inch-thick wall. Fill each potato with about ½ cup of corned beef hash.

**3.** Place filled potatoes on lightly greased baking sheet. Bake 55 minutes or until tender when pierced with fork.

**4.** Prepare eggs as desired. Arrange on top of potatoes. *Makes 4 servings*

# BREAKFAST BASICS

## POPOVERS

**3 eggs**
**1 cup milk**
**1 tablespoon butter or margarine, melted**
**1 cup all-purpose flour**
**¼ teaspoon salt**

**1.** Preheat oven to 375°F. Grease 12 muffin cups or 6 custard cups.

**2.** Beat eggs, milk and butter in medium bowl. Add flour and salt; beat until smooth.

**3.** Pour batter into prepared cups, filling about ¾ full. (If using custard cups, place on baking sheet.) Bake 45 to 50 minutes or until brown and crispy. Serve immediately.

*Makes 12 small or 6 large popovers*

**CHEESE POPOVERS:** Add ⅛ teaspoon garlic powder and ¼ cup grated Parmesan cheese to batter. Bake as above.

## PUFF PANCAKE WITH SUMMER BERRIES

**2 eggs**
**½ cup all-purpose flour**
**½ cup milk**
**2 tablespoons butter or margarine, melted**
**1 tablespoon sugar**
**¼ teaspoon salt**
**Summer Berries (recipe follows)**

**1.** Preheat oven to 425°F. Grease 10-inch ovenproof skillet.

**2.** With electric mixer, beat eggs. Add flour, milk, butter, sugar and salt; beat until smooth.

**3.** Pour batter into prepared skillet. Bake 15 minutes.

**4.** *Reduce oven temperature to 350°F.* Continue baking 10 to 15 minutes or until puffed and golden brown.

**5.** Serve pancake in skillet with Summer Berries.

*Makes 6 servings*

Summer Berries
**2 cups blueberries**
**1 cup sliced strawberries**
**1 cup raspberries**
**Sugar to taste**
**Cream (optional)**

Combine blueberries, strawberries and raspberries in medium bowl. Gently toss with sugar. Let stand 5 minutes. Top with cream if desired.

BREAKFAST BASICS

## BAKED EGGS

**4 eggs**
**4 teaspoons milk**
**Salt and freshly ground pepper to taste**

**1.** Preheat oven to 375°F. Grease 4 small baking dishes or custard cups.

**2.** Break 1 egg into each dish. Add 1 teaspoon milk to each dish. Season with salt and pepper.

**3.** Bake about 15 minutes or until set.

*Makes 4 servings*

---

### Baked Egg Options

*Top eggs with desired amount of one or more of the following before baking; continue as above.*

| | |
|---|---|
| *Light cream* | *Chopped ham* |
| *Salsa* | *Minced chives* |
| *Shredded cheese* | *Minced fresh herbs* |

---

## BAKING POWDER BISCUITS

**2 cups all-purpose flour**
**1 tablespoon baking powder**
**½ teaspoon salt**
**¼ cup butter or margarine**
**3 tablespoons shortening**
**About ¾ cup milk**

**1.** Preheat oven to 450°F. Grease baking sheet.

**2.** Sift flour, baking powder and salt into medium bowl. Using pastry blender or 2 knives, cut in butter and shortening until mixture resembles coarse crumbs. Stir in enough milk to make soft dough.

**3.** Turn out onto lightly floured surface. Knead dough lightly. Roll out ½ inch thick. Cut biscuit rounds with 2-inch cutter. Place on greased baking sheet.

**4.** Bake 8 to 10 minutes or until browned.

*Makes 16 biscuits*

**DROP BISCUITS:** Make dough as above, increasing milk to about 1 cup or enough to make stiff batter. Drop by tablespoonfuls onto greased baking sheet. Bake 5 to 8 minutes or until browned. *Makes about 28 biscuits*

*Baked Eggs*

BREAKFAST BASICS

## SANTA FE POTATO CAKES

**3 cups** *cooked* **instant mashed potato flakes
     or leftover unbuttered mashed potatoes**
**1 can (4 ounces) diced green chiles, drained**
**⅔ cup cornmeal, divided**
**3 green onions, sliced**
**⅓ cup (about 1½ ounces) shredded Cheddar
     cheese**
**2 eggs, beaten**
**2 tablespoons chopped fresh cilantro**
**1 teaspoon chili powder**
**½ teaspoon LAWRY'S® Seasoned Salt**
**½ teaspoon LAWRY'S® Seasoned Pepper**
**2 tablespoons olive oil, divided**
    **Salsa**
    **Dairy sour cream**

In large bowl, combine potatoes, chiles, ½ cup
cornmeal, onions, cheese, eggs, cilantro, chili
powder, Seasoned Salt and Seasoned Pepper; shape
into eight patties. Sprinkle both sides with
remaining cornmeal; set aside. In large nonstick
skillet, heat 1 tablespoon oil over medium heat.
Add four patties; cook 5 to 7 minutes or until
golden brown, turning once. Remove from skillet;
keep warm. Repeat with remaining oil and patties.
Garnish as desired.          *Makes 4 servings*

**PRESENTATION:** Serve with salsa and sour
cream.

## CREAMY OATMEAL

**1⅓ cups old-fashioned rolled oats**
**3 cups milk**
**½ cup raisins**
**4 teaspoons sugar**
**⅛ teaspoon salt**

**1.** Combine oats, milk, raisins, sugar and salt in
medium saucepan over medium heat.

**2.** Bring to a boil, stirring occasionally. Reduce
heat and simmer 5 minutes. Cover; remove from
heat. Let stand 5 minutes.          *Makes 4 servings*

---

*For a quick, make-ahead breakfast, freeze
oatmeal in individual portions. It can be reheated
quickly in the microwave, saving the fuss of
measuring, cooking and cleaning up.*

*Santa Fe Potato Cakes*

# BREAKFAST BASICS

## SUNRISE PANCAKES

    **Vanilla Cream Syrup (recipe follows)**
**1 cup all-purpose flour**
**2 tablespoons sugar**
**1 teaspoon baking powder**
**½ teaspoon baking soda**
**½ teaspoon salt**
**2 eggs, slightly beaten**
**½ cup plain yogurt**
**½ cup water**
**2 tablespoons butter or margarine, melted**

**1.** Prepare Vanilla Cream Syrup; set aside.

**2.** Combine flour, sugar, baking powder, baking soda and salt in large bowl.

**3.** Combine eggs, yogurt and water in medium bowl. Whisk in butter. Pour liquid ingredients, all at once, into dry ingredients; stir until moistened.

**4.** Preheat griddle or large skillet over medium heat; grease lightly. Pour about ¼ cup batter onto hot griddle for each pancake; spread batter out to make 5-inch circles. Cook until tops of pancakes are bubbly and appear dry; turn and cook until browned, about 2 minutes.

*Makes about 8 pancakes*

Vanilla Cream Syrup
    **½ cup sugar**
    **½ cup light corn syrup**
    **½ cup whipping cream**
    **1 teaspoon vanilla**
    **1 nectarine, diced**

Combine sugar, corn syrup and cream in 1-quart pan. Cook, stirring constantly, over medium heat until sugar is dissolved. Simmer 2 minutes or until syrup thickens slightly. Remove from heat. Stir in vanilla and nectarine. *Makes 1 cup*

## SAUSAGE GRAVY

    **¼ pound spicy bulk sausage**
    **¼ cup all-purpose flour**
    **2 cups milk**
    **½ teaspoon salt**
    **¼ teaspoon freshly ground pepper**

**1.** Cook sausage in medium saucepan over medium heat until browned, stirring to crumble.

**2.** Drain off all fat except about 2 tablespoons. Stir in flour. Cook, stirring constantly, until thickened and bubbly.

**3.** Gradually whisk in milk, salt and pepper. Cook, stirring constantly, until thickened and bubbly, about 5 minutes. *Makes about 4 servings*

*Sunrise Pancakes*

# BREAKFAST BASICS

## CHEESY CORN BAKE

3 eggs, well beaten
1 can (16 ounces) creamed corn
¾ cup unseasoned dry bread crumbs
¾ cup (3 ounces) shredded Cheddar cheese
½ cup hot milk
½ medium-sized green bell pepper, chopped
3 teaspoons chopped onion
1 teaspoon LAWRY'S® Seasoned Salt
¾ teaspoon LAWRY'S® Seasoned Pepper
¼ teaspoon LAWRY'S® Garlic Powder with Parsley

Preheat oven to 350°F. In large bowl, combine eggs, corn, bread crumbs, cheese, milk, bell pepper, onion, Seasoned Salt, Seasoned Pepper and Garlic Powder with Parsley. Pour into ungreased 2-quart casserole. Bake in 350°F oven 1 hour. Let stand 10 minutes before serving.          *Makes 6 servings*

**HINT:** Serve topped with prepared LAWRY'S® Original Style Spaghetti Sauce for extra flavor.

## COUNTRY BREAKFAST SAUSAGE

1 pound ground pork
1 teaspoon ground cumin
½ teaspoon dried thyme leaves
½ teaspoon rubbed sage
1 teaspoon salt
½ teaspoon freshly ground black pepper
⅛ teaspoon ground red (cayenne) pepper (optional)

**1.** Combine pork, cumin, thyme, sage, salt, black pepper and ground red pepper in medium bowl; mix well. Cover and refrigerate overnight for flavors to blend.

**2.** Shape into 6 patties. Cook in lightly greased skillet over medium heat about 15 minutes or until browned on both sides and centers are no longer pink, turning occasionally.          *Makes 6 servings*

*Cheesy Corn Bake*

**BREAKFAST BASICS**

## POTATO-CARROT PANCAKES

  1 pound russet potatoes, peeled
  1 medium carrot, peeled
  2 tablespoons minced green onion
  1 tablespoon all-purpose flour
  1 egg, beaten
  ½ teaspoon salt
  ⅛ teaspoon freshly ground pepper
  2 tablespoons vegetable oil

**1.** Shred potatoes and carrot into medium bowl. Squeeze out excess moisture.

**2.** Add green onion, flour, egg, salt and pepper; mix well.

**3.** Heat oil in large skillet over medium heat. Drop spoonfuls of potato mixture into skillet; flatten to form thin circles.

**4.** Cook until browned on bottom; turn pancakes and cook until potatoes are tender, about 10 minutes total cooking time.

*Makes about 12 pancakes*

## CRÊPES

  ¾ cup all-purpose flour
  3 eggs
  1 cup milk
  3 tablespoons butter or margarine, melted
  ½ teaspoon salt
    About 2 tablespoons vegetable oil

**1.** Combine flour, eggs, milk, butter and salt in blender or food processor. Cover; process until combined. Cover and refrigerate at least 1 hour.

**2.** Brush 7-inch skillet with oil. Place over medium heat until hot. Add 3 tablespoons crêpe batter, tilting skillet to cover bottom evenly.

**3.** Cook until golden brown on bottom; turn over. Cook until browned on underside.

**4.** Stack crêpes between waxed paper squares to prevent sticking together. Repeat with remaining batter, oiling skillet occasionally.

*Makes 16 crêpes*

**TIP:** Stacked crêpes can be placed in plastic food storage bag and refrigerated 2 to 3 days or frozen up to 1 month. Thaw before using.

*Potato-Carrot Pancakes*

# — *Zippy* —

## BREAKFASTS IN A FLASH

### PITA IN THE MORNING

1 teaspoon butter or margarine
2 eggs, lightly beaten
¼ teaspoon salt
   Dash pepper
1 whole wheat pita bread, cut in half
¼ cup alfalfa sprouts
2 tablespoons shredded Cheddar cheese
2 tablespoons chopped tomato
   Avocado slices (optional)

**1.** Melt butter at HIGH (100%) 30 seconds in microwave-safe 1-quart casserole.

**2.** Season eggs with salt and pepper. Add eggs to casserole. Microwave at HIGH 1½ to 2½ minutes, stirring once. Do not overcook; eggs should be soft with no liquid remaining.

**3.** Open pita to make pockets. Arrange sprouts in pockets. Divide cheese and eggs evenly between pockets. Top with tomato and avocado slices.     *Makes 1 sandwich*

BREAKFASTS IN A FLASH

# BAGEL TOPPERS

Orange-Cream Bagel Spread
**1 package (8 ounces) cream cheese,
    softened**
**3 tablespoons orange marmalade**

Combine cream cheese and marmalade in small
bowl.                           *Makes about 1 cup*

Chocolate-Cream Bagel Spread
**1 package (8 ounces) cream cheese,
    softened**
**3 ounces white chocolate, melted**
**2 tablespoons mini chocolate chips**

Combine cream cheese and white chocolate in
small bowl. Stir in chocolate chips.
                        *Makes about 1¼ cups*

Crab Bagel Spread
**4 ounces cream cheese, softened**
**2 ounces crabmeat, shredded**
**2 tablespoons chopped green onion tops**
**4 teaspoons lemon juice**
**1 tablespoon milk**

Combine cream cheese, crabmeat, onion tops,
lemon juice and milk in medium bowl.
                        *Makes about ¾ cup*

Peanut Butter Topper
**2 tablespoons creamy peanut butter**
**1 tablespoon raisins**
**1 small banana, thinly sliced**
**1 tablespoon sunflower kernels**

Spread bagel with peanut butter. Top with raisins,
banana slices and sunflower kernels.
                        *Makes 1 to 2 servings*

*No time for breakfast? Prepare a bagel topper
the night before. Experiment with your
favorite fruits and vegetables to produce
your own fantastic flavors!*

**Bagel Toppers (left to right):** *Crab Bagel Spread
and Peanut Butter Topper*

## BREAKFASTS IN A FLASH

## TROPICAL TURKEY MELT

**1 English muffin, split**
**1 teaspoon Dijon-style mustard**
**3 ounces smoked turkey slices**
**3 thin slices papaya**
**1 slice Monterey Jack cheese**
**Butter or margarine, softened**

**1.** Spread inside of muffin halves with mustard. On 1 half, layer turkey, papaya and cheese. Press remaining muffin half, mustard-side down, over cheese.

**2.** Spread butter on outsides of muffin halves.

**3.** Cook sandwich in small skillet over medium heat until toasted, about 4 minutes; turn and cook on remaining side until toasted and cheese is melted. Serve hot. *Makes 1 serving*

## CEREAL TRAIL MIX

**¼ cup butter or margarine**
**2 tablespoons sugar**
**1 teaspoon ground cinnamon**
**1 cup bite-sized oat cereal squares**
**1 cup bite-sized wheat cereal squares**
**1 cup bite-sized rice cereal squares**
**¼ cup toasted slivered almonds**
**¾ cup raisins**

**1.** Melt butter at HIGH (100%) 1½ minutes in large microwave-safe bowl. Add sugar and cinnamon; mix well. Add cereals and nuts; stir to coat.

**2.** Microwave at HIGH 2 minutes. Stir well. Microwave 2 minutes more; stir well. Add raisins. Microwave an additional 2 to 3 minutes, stirring well after 2 minutes. Spread on paper towels; mix will become crisp as it cools. Store tightly covered. *Makes about 4 cups*

*Tropical Turkey Melt*

BREAKFASTS IN A FLASH

## BREAKFAST PARFAIT

**½ cup Date-Nut Granola (page 12) or your
   favorite granola
¼ cup plain nonfat yogurt or cottage cheese
½ cup sliced strawberries
½ ripe banana, sliced**

Place half of granola in parfait glass or glass bowl.
Top with half of yogurt. Arrange half of
strawberries and the banana over yogurt. Top with
remaining granola, yogurt and strawberries.

*Makes 1 serving*

---

### Vitamin C

*The morning meal is a good  time to get your
daily dose of vitamin C. Good sources include
orange, grapefruit and tomato juices and
strawberries, cantaloupe and kiwifruit.*

---

## DANISH BAGEL

**1 raisin or blueberry bagel, halved
½ cup ricotta cheese
8 teaspoons Cinnamon Sugar (recipe
   follows), divided
1 peach, thinly sliced**

1. Preheat broiler.

2. Spread bagel halves with ricotta. Sprinkle each
half with 2 teaspoons Cinnamon Sugar. Arrange
peach slices over cheese. Sprinkle with remaining
Cinnamon Sugar.

3. Place bagel halves on baking sheet. Broil 6
inches from heat, about 4 minutes, until sugar is
bubbly and mixture is hot. Serve warm.

*Makes 2 servings*

**CINNAMON SUGAR:** Combine ½ cup sugar
with 1 tablespoon ground cinnamon. Store in
shaker-top jar.

*Breakfast Parfaits*

# BREAKFAST IN A GLASS

Raspberry Lemon Smoothie
- **1 cup frozen raspberries**
- **1 carton (8 ounces) lemon-flavored yogurt**
- **½ cup milk**
- **1 teaspoon vanilla**

Place all ingredients in blender. Cover; process until smooth. *Makes about 1½ cups*

Berry-Banana Breakfast Smoothie
- **1 carton (8 ounces) berry-flavored yogurt**
- **1 ripe banana, cut into chunks**
- **½ cup milk**

Place all ingredients in blender. Cover; process until smooth. *Makes about 2 cups*

Peanut Butter-Banana Shake
- **1 cup milk**
- **½ cup vanilla ice cream**
- **1 ripe banana, cut into chunks**
- **2 tablespoons peanut butter**

Place all ingredients in blender. Cover; process until smooth. *Makes about 2 cups*

Mocha Cooler
- **1 cup milk**
- **¼ cup vanilla or coffee ice cream**
- **1 tablespoon instant coffee granules**
- **1 tablespoon chocolate syrup**

Place all ingredients in blender. Cover; process until smooth. *Makes about 1½ cups*

Rise 'n' Shine Shake
- **1 cup milk**
- **1 cup strawberries, hulled**
- **1 kiwifruit, peeled and quartered**
- **¼ cup vanilla or strawberry frozen yogurt**
- **1 to 2 tablespoons sugar**

Place all ingredients in blender. Cover; process until smooth. *Makes about 1½ cups*

Peachy Banana Shake
- **1 cup milk**
- **½ cup vanilla ice cream**
- **1 ripe banana, cut into chunks**
- **1 peach, pitted and sliced**
- **1 teaspoon vanilla extract**

Place all ingredients in blender. Cover; process until smooth. *Makes about 2 cups*

Mango Yogurt Drink
- **½ cup plain yogurt**
- **1 ripe mango, peeled, seeded and sliced**
- **¼ cup orange juice**
- **1 teaspoon honey**
- **2 ice cubes**
- **Milk (optional)**

Place all ingredients in blender. Cover; process until smooth. Add milk to obtain preferred consistency. *Makes about 1½ cups*

**TIP:** The skin of most mangoes tinges with more red or yellow as the fruit ripens. Mangoes are ready to eat when they yield to gentle pressure.

## BREAKFASTS IN A FLASH

## MINI SAUSAGE BISCUIT SANDWICHES

**1 package (1 pound) LOUIS RICH® fully cooked Turkey Smoked Sausage**
**2 cans (10 ounces each) refrigerated buttermilk flaky biscuits**
**Honey, barbecue sauce or ketchup (optional)**

Preheat oven to 400°F. Cut sausage lengthwise in half; cut each half again in half lengthwise. Cut each quarter into 5 pieces. Remove biscuits from can; separate. Using fingers, flatten each biscuit to 4-inch diameter.

Place small amount of honey, barbecue sauce or ketchup, if desired, in center of each biscuit; top each with 1 piece of sausage. Bring up edges of biscuit and pinch together to seal over top of sausage. Place on baking sheet. Bake about 10 minutes or until lightly browned.

*Makes 20 mini sandwiches*

## DELUXE TURKEY PITA MELT

**1 whole wheat pita bread**
**2 ounces Brie or other soft cheese**
**2 ounces sliced smoked turkey**
**1 medium tomato, thinly sliced**
**¼ teaspoon dried basil leaves**
**Alfalfa sprouts or shredded lettuce**

**1.** Preheat oven to 400°F. Cut pita around edge to make 2 flat pieces.

**2.** Spread inside of each pita half with Brie. Top with turkey, tomato and basil.

**3.** Place pita halves on baking sheet. Bake about 5 minutes or until cheese melts and topping is hot.

**4.** Remove from oven; top with alfalfa sprouts. Serve warm.

*Makes 2 servings*

# BREAKFAST RICE

1 bag SUCCESS® Rice
1 carton (8 ounces) Dutch apple nonfat
    yogurt
¼ cup raisins
¼ cup chopped nuts
1 teaspoon cinnamon
    Apple juice (optional)

Prepare rice according to package directions. Cool.

Combine rice with yogurt, raisins, nuts and cinnamon in medium bowl; mix well. Chill. When ready to serve, add a small amount of apple juice to moisten, if desired. Garnish, if desired.

*Makes 4 servings*

---

### A Nutritious Breakfast

*Nutritionists suggest you include foods from three of the four food groups for a healthy breakfast. The four food groups are: milk and other dairy products, fruits and vegetables, breads and cereals and meat and other protein foods (including fish, poultry, cheese, nuts, eggs, dried peas and beans).*

---

# EGGS DANNON®

4 eggs
4 thin slices Canadian bacon
1 cup DANNON® Plain Nonfat or Lowfat
    Yogurt
½ teaspoon dry mustard
    Dash ground red pepper
2 English muffins, split and toasted

Spray a large skillet with vegetable cooking spray. Fill half full with water. Bring to a boil; reduce heat until water simmers. Break 1 egg into a small dish and slide into water. Repeat with remaining eggs. Simmer 3 to 5 minutes or until yolks are firm.

In a separate large skillet over medium-high heat cook bacon 3 to 4 minutes or until heated through, turning once; set aside. In a small saucepan whisk together yogurt, mustard and red pepper. Cook and stir over low heat just until warm. *Do not boil.* Top each English muffin half with bacon slice, egg and ¼ cup sauce. Serve immediately.

*4 servings*

*Breakfast Rice*

*BREAKFASTS IN A FLASH*

## SPICY SAUSAGE SKILLET BREAKFAST

**2 bags SUCCESS® Rice**
   **Vegetable cooking spray**
**1 pound bulk turkey sausage**
**½ cup chopped onion**
**1 can (10 ounces) tomatoes with green chilies, undrained**
**1 tablespoon chili powder**
**1 cup (4 ounces) shredded reduced-fat Monterey Jack cheese**

Prepare rice according to package directions.

Lightly spray large skillet with cooking spray. Crumble sausage into prepared skillet. Cook over medium heat until lightly browned, stirring occasionally. Add onion; cook until tender. Stir in tomatoes, chili powder and rice; simmer 2 minutes. Reduce heat to low. Simmer until no liquid remains, about 8 minutes, stirring occasionally. Sprinkle with cheese.        *Makes 6 to 8 servings*

## MICROWAVED OATS CEREAL

**1¾ cups water**
**⅓ cup old-fashioned rolled oats**
**⅓ cup oat bran**
**1 tablespoon brown sugar**
**¼ teaspoon ground cinnamon**
**⅛ teaspoon salt**

**1.** Combine water, oats, oat bran, sugar, cinnamon and salt in large microwave-safe bowl (cereal expands rapidly when it cooks). Cover with plastic wrap; vent.

**2.** Microwave on HIGH (100%) about 6 minutes or until thickened. Stir well. Let stand 2 minutes before serving.        *Makes 2 servings*

*Add some excitement to your oatmeal by stirring in peanut butter, mashed bananas or molasses. (Or maybe all three!)*

*Spicy Sausage Skillet Breakfast*

BREAKFASTS IN A FLASH

## BANANA BERRY BLEND

**1 cup DANNON® Plain Nonfat or Lowfat Yogurt**
**½ cup orange juice**
**½ cup fresh or frozen unsweetened strawberries**
**1 ripe banana, sliced**
**2 tablespoons honey**
**1 tablespoon wheat germ (optional)**

In blender combine yogurt, orange juice, strawberries, banana, honey and wheat germ. Cover and blend on high speed until smooth. Serve immediately over ice or in frosted mugs.

*2 servings*

---

*Start your day with a super-easy blender drink. Create your own smoothie recipe using your three favorite fruits!*

---

## SUNRISE BURRITO

**2 ounces bulk sausage**
**¼ cup chopped onion**
**2 eggs**
**1 tablespoon water**
**2 tablespoons canned chopped green chilies**
**1 (10-inch) flour tortilla**

**1.** Combine sausage and onion in microwave-safe 1-quart casserole. Microwave at HIGH (100%) 1½ to 2½ minutes or until sausage is brown and onion is tender, stirring once to break up meat.

**2.** Beat eggs with water in small bowl. Stir in chilies.

**3.** Drain fat from casserole. Add egg mixture to sausage and onion; mix well. Microwave at HIGH 1½ to 2½ minutes, stirring once. Do not overcook; eggs should be soft with no liquid remaining.

**4.** Microwave tortilla at HIGH about 15 seconds. Fill with scrambled egg mixture.

*Makes 1 burrito*

**TIP:** To heat tortilla in a microwave oven, wrap loosely in a damp paper towel before microwaving.

*Banana Berry Blend*

# EGG ENTRÉES

## EGG BLOSSOMS

**4 sheets phyllo pastry**
**2 tablespoons butter, melted**
**4 teaspoons grated Parmesan cheese**
**4 eggs**
**4 teaspoons minced green onion**
  **Salt and freshly ground pepper**
  **Tomato Sauce (page 44)**

**1.** Preheat oven to 350°F. Grease 4 (2½-inch) muffin cups. Brush 1 sheet of phyllo with butter. Top with another sheet; brush with butter. Cut stack into 6 (4-inch) squares. Repeat with remaining 2 sheets. Stack 3 squares together, rotating so corners do not overlap. Press into greased muffin cup. Repeat with remaining squares.

**2.** Sprinkle 1 teaspoon cheese into each phyllo-lined cup. Break 1 egg into each cup. Sprinkle onion over eggs. Season with salt and pepper. Bake 15 to 20 minutes or until pastry is golden and eggs are set. Serve with Tomato Sauce.

*Makes 4 servings*

*continued*

EGG ENTRÉES

Tomato Sauce

   **1 can (16 ounces) whole tomatoes, undrained, chopped**
   **1 clove garlic, minced**
   **½ cup chopped onion**
   **1 tablespoon white wine vinegar**
   **½ teaspoon salt**
   **¼ teaspoon dried oregano leaves**

Combine tomatoes, garlic, onion, vinegar, salt and oregano in medium saucepan. Cook, stirring occasionally, over medium heat until onion is tender, about 20 minutes. Serve warm.

---

*Trying to lose weight? Don't skip breakfast! When you neglect this very important meal, you are more likely to overeat at lunch, dinner or in-between.*

---

## BREAKFAST IN A LOAF

   **1 round loaf bread (8 to 9 inches)**
   **4 ounces sliced ham**
   **½ red bell pepper, thinly sliced crosswise**
   **½ cup (2 ounces) shredded Monterey Jack cheese**
   **½ cup (2 ounces) shredded Cheddar cheese**
   **1 recipe Scrambled Eggs (page 14)**
   **½ cup sliced ripe olives**
   **1 medium tomato, thinly sliced**
   **8 ounces mushrooms, sliced, cooked**

**1.** Preheat oven to 350°F. Cut 2-inch slice from top of loaf; set aside for lid. Remove soft interior of loaf, leaving a 1-inch-thick wall and bottom.

**2.** Place ham in bottom of loaf. Top with bell pepper rings; sprinkle with half of cheeses. Layer Scrambled Eggs, olives and tomato over cheeses. Top with remaining cheeses and mushrooms.

**3.** Place lid on loaf. Wrap in foil. Place on baking sheet. Bake about 30 minutes or until heated through. Cut into 8 wedges.    *Makes 8 servings*

*Breakfast in a Loaf*

## EGG ENTRÉES

## MUSHROOM & ONION EGG BAKE

   1 tablespoon vegetable oil
   4 green onions, chopped
   4 ounces mushrooms, sliced
   1 cup low fat cottage cheese
   1 cup sour cream
   6 eggs
   2 tablespoons all-purpose flour
   ¼ teaspoon salt
   ⅛ teaspoon freshly ground pepper
     Dash hot pepper sauce

**1.** Preheat oven to 350°F. Grease shallow 1-quart baking dish.

**2.** Heat oil in medium skillet over medium heat. Add onions and mushrooms; cook until tender. Set aside.

**3.** In blender or food processor, process cottage cheese until almost smooth. Add sour cream, eggs, flour, salt, pepper and hot pepper sauce; process until combined. Stir in onions and mushrooms. Pour into greased dish. Bake about 40 minutes or until knife inserted near center comes out clean.

*Makes about 6 servings*

## FRESH STRAWBERRY BANANA OMELETS

   1 cup sliced strawberries
   1 banana, sliced
   4 teaspoons sugar
   ¼ teaspoon grated lemon peel
   1 tablespoon lemon juice
   4 eggs
   ¼ cup water
   ¼ teaspoon salt
   2 tablespoons butter or margarine, divided

**1.** Combine strawberries, banana, sugar, lemon peel and juice in medium bowl; mix lightly. Cover; let stand 15 minutes at room temperature.

**2.** Combine eggs, water and salt in small bowl. Melt 1 tablespoon butter in 8-inch omelet pan or skillet over medium heat.

**3.** Add ½ egg mixture (about ½ cup). Lift cooked edges with spatula to allow uncooked eggs to flow under cooked portion. Shake pan to loosen omelet.

**4.** Cook until almost set; add ½ cup fruit filling. Fold in half. Turn out onto plate. Keep warm. Repeat with remaining butter and egg mixture. Top with remaining fruit filling.

*Makes 2 servings*

*Top to bottom: Country Breakfast Sausage (page 22) and Mushroom & Onion Egg Bake*

**EGG ENTRÉES**

# EGGS RANCHEROS

**RANCHERO SAUCE**
   **1 can (16 ounces) whole tomatoes, undrained, chopped**
   **1 can (4 ounces) chopped green chilies, drained**
   **½ cup chopped onion**
   **1 tablespoon white wine vinegar**
   **¼ teaspoon salt**

**EGGS**
   **1 tablespoon vegetable oil**
   **4 eggs**
   **Salt and pepper to taste**
   **1 can (30 ounces) refried beans**
   **1 cup (4 ounces) shredded Cheddar cheese**
   **4 corn tortillas**

**1.** For Ranchero Sauce, combine tomatoes, chilies, onion, vinegar and salt in medium saucepan. Cook, stirring occasionally, over medium heat until onion is tender, about 20 minutes. Keep warm.

**2.** For eggs, heat oil in large skillet over medium-low heat. Break eggs into skillet. Season with salt and pepper. Cook 2 to 3 minutes or until eggs are set. Turn eggs for over-easy eggs.

**3.** Heat beans in medium saucepan. Spoon beans onto 4 warmed plates; sprinkle evenly with cheese.

**4.** Heat tortillas. Place 1 tortilla on each plate; top each tortilla with 1 egg. Spoon warm Ranchero Sauce over eggs. *Makes 4 servings*

**TIP:** To heat tortillas in a conventional oven, wrap in foil and place in 350°F oven about 10 minutes. To heat tortillas in a microwave oven, wrap loosely in a damp paper towel. Heat on HIGH (100%) about 1 minute.

---

*Cooking Eggs*

*When cooking eggs, remember that too high a temperature will cause them to be tough and rubbery. Use either low or medium heat.*

---

*Eggs Rancheros*

# EGG ENTRÉES

## SPANISH POTATO OMELET

¼ **cup olive oil**
¼ **cup vegetable oil**
1 **pound thin-skinned red or white potatoes, cut into ⅛-inch slices**
½ **teaspoon salt, divided**
1 **small onion, cut in half lengthwise, thinly sliced crosswise**
¼ **cup chopped green bell pepper**
¼ **cup chopped red bell pepper**
3 **eggs**

**1.** Heat oils in large skillet over medium-high heat. Add potatoes to hot oil. Turn with spatula several times to coat all slices with oil.

**2.** Sprinkle with ¼ teaspoon salt. Cook 6 to 9 minutes or until potatoes become translucent, turning occasionally. Add onion and peppers. Reduce heat to medium.

**3.** Cook 10 minutes or until potatoes are tender, turning occasionally. Drain mixture in colander placed in large bowl; reserve oil. Let potato mixture stand until cool.

**4.** Beat eggs with remaining ¼ teaspoon salt in large bowl. Gently stir in potato mixture; lightly press into bowl until mixture is covered with eggs. Let stand 15 minutes.

**5.** Heat 2 teaspoons reserved oil in 6-inch skillet over medium-high heat. Spread potato mixture in pan to form solid layer. Cook until egg on bottom and side of pan is set but top still looks moist.

**6.** Cover pan with plate. Flip omelet onto plate, then slide omelet back into pan uncooked side down. Continue to cook until bottom is lightly browned.

**7.** Slide omelet onto serving plate. Let stand 30 minutes before serving. Cut into 8 wedges to serve.
*Makes 8 servings*

## STUFFED TOMATOES & CREAMED SPINACH

4 **medium tomatoes**
¼ **cup grated Parmesan cheese**
4 **eggs**
4 **teaspoons minced green onion**
**Salt and freshly ground pepper to taste**
**Creamed Spinach (page 51)**

**1.** Preheat oven to 375°F.

**2.** Cut thin slice off blossom end of each tomato; remove seeds and pulp, being careful not to pierce side of tomato. Place tomato shells in shallow baking dish.

**3.** Sprinkle 1 tablespoon Parmesan cheese inside each tomato. Break an egg into each tomato. Top with onion, salt and pepper. Bake 15 to 20 minutes or until eggs are set. Serve with Creamed Spinach.
*Makes 4 servings*

# EGG ENTRÉES

### Creamed Spinach

1 package (10 ounces) frozen chopped
    spinach, thawed
2 tablespoons butter or margarine
2 tablespoons all-purpose flour
1 cup milk
¼ teaspoon salt
    Dash freshly ground pepper
1 tablespoon grated Parmesan cheese
    (optional)

**1.** Press spinach to remove all moisture; set aside. Melt butter in medium saucepan over medium heat. Stir in flour; cook until bubbly.

**2.** Slowly stir in milk. Cook until thickened. Add spinach; continue cooking over low heat, stirring constantly, about 5 minutes or until spinach is tender. Season with salt, pepper and cheese.

## EASY CRAB-ASPARAGUS PIE

4 ounces crabmeat, shredded
12 ounces fresh asparagus, cooked
½ cup chopped onion, cooked
1 cup (4 ounces) shredded Monterey Jack
    cheese
¼ cup grated Parmesan cheese
    Freshly ground pepper
¾ cup all-purpose flour
¾ teaspoon baking powder
½ teaspoon salt
2 tablespoons butter or margarine, chilled
1½ cups milk
4 eggs

**1.** Preheat oven to 350°F. Lightly grease 10-inch quiche dish or pie plate.

**2.** Layer crabmeat, asparagus and onion in prepared pie plate. Top with cheeses. Season with pepper.

**3.** Combine flour, baking powder and salt in large bowl. With pastry blender or 2 knives, cut in butter. Add milk and eggs; stir until blended. Pour over vegetables and cheeses.

**4.** Bake about 30 minutes or until filling is puffed and knife inserted near center comes out clean. Serve hot.     *Makes 6 servings*

# EGG ENTRÉES

## ROASTED VEGETABLE OMELET WITH FRESH SALSA

**Fresh Salsa (recipe follows)**
**4 small red potatoes, scrubbed and cut into quarters**
**⅓ cup coarsely chopped red bell pepper**
**2 slices bacon, chopped**
**1 medium green onion, cut into thin slices**
**3 eggs**
**1 tablespoon water**
**Salt and black pepper to taste**
**1 tablespoon butter or margarine**
**⅓ cup shredded Colby cheese**
**Fresh cilantro sprigs for garnish**

**1.** Prepare Fresh Salsa. Preheat oven to 425°F.

**2.** Combine potatoes, bell pepper, bacon and green onion in greased 15×10-inch jelly-roll pan. Bake 30 minutes or until potatoes are tender, stirring occasionally.

**3.** Beat eggs, water, salt and black pepper with fork or wire whisk in small bowl.

**4.** Melt butter in 10-inch skillet over medium-high heat. Pour egg mixture into skillet; cook until eggs begin to set. Gently lift up sides of omelet with spatula to allow liquid to run under bottom of omelet.

**5.** When omelet is set, but not dry, and bottom is a light golden brown, remove from heat. Place roasted vegetable mixture over ½ of omelet; sprinkle with cheese. Gently fold omelet in half with spatula. Transfer to serving plate. Serve with Fresh Salsa. Garnish, if desired.

*Makes 2 servings*

Fresh Salsa
**3 medium plum tomatoes, seeded and chopped**
**2 tablespoons chopped onion**
**1 small jalapeño pepper, stemmed, seeded and minced***
**1 tablespoon chopped fresh cilantro**
**1 tablespoon lime juice**
**¼ teaspoon salt**
**⅛ teaspoon black pepper**

Combine tomatoes, onion, jalapeño pepper, cilantro, lime juice, salt and black pepper; mix well. Refrigerate until ready to use.

*Jalapeño peppers can sting and irritate the skin; wear rubber gloves when handling and do not touch eyes. Wash hands after handling jalapeño peppers.

*Roasted Vegetable Omelet with Fresh Salsa*

# EGG ENTRÉES

## CALIFORNIA CROISSANTS

  1 teaspoon vinegar*
  4 eggs
  2 croissants, halved and toasted
  4 slices tomato
  ½ avocado, sliced crosswise
  8 slices crisp-cooked bacon
    Mornay Sauce (recipe follows)
    Chopped chives and sprouts

**1.** Fill wide saucepan or deep skillet with about 1½ inches water. Add vinegar. Bring to a simmer. Break 1 egg into shallow cup or saucer. Gently slide egg into simmering water. Repeat with remaining eggs.

**2.** Cook eggs 3 to 4 minutes or until set. Carefully remove eggs with slotted spoon; drain on paper towels.

**3.** Place croissant half on each plate. Layer tomato, avocado and bacon on croissant. Top with poached eggs. Divide Mornay Sauce equally among croissants. Garnish with chives and sprouts.

*Makes 4 servings*

*Adding vinegar to the water helps keep the egg white intact while poaching.

### Mornay Sauce

  2 tablespoons butter or margarine
  2 tablespoons all-purpose flour
1½ cups milk
  ¼ cup (1 ounce) shredded Cheddar cheese
  2 tablespoons grated Parmesan cheese
  ½ teaspoon Dijon-style mustard
  ¼ teaspoon salt
  ⅛ teaspoon white pepper

**1.** Melt butter in medium saucepan over medium heat. Add flour; stir until bubbly.

**2.** Gradually stir in milk. Cook, stirring constantly, until mixture comes to a boil. Continue cooking until thickened.

**3.** Stir in cheeses, mustard, salt and pepper. Remove from heat and continue stirring until cheese melts.          *Makes about 1¾ cups*

*California Croissant*

# EGG ENTRÉES

## ARTICHOKE FRITTATA

**1 can (14 ounces) artichoke hearts, drained
   and rinsed
Olive oil
½ cup minced green onions
5 eggs
½ cup (2 ounces) shredded Swiss cheese
2 tablespoons grated Parmesan cheese
1 tablespoon minced fresh savory *or*
   1 teaspoon dried savory leaves
1 tablespoon minced fresh parsley
1 teaspoon salt
Freshly ground pepper to taste**

**1.** Chop artichoke hearts; set aside.

**2.** Heat 1 tablespoon olive oil in 10-inch skillet over medium heat. Add green onions; cook until tender. Remove with slotted spoon; set aside.

**3.** Beat eggs in medium bowl until light. Stir in artichokes, green onions, cheeses, herbs, salt and pepper.

**4.** Heat 1½ teaspoons olive oil in same skillet over medium heat. Pour egg mixture into skillet.

**5.** Cook 4 to 5 minutes or until bottom is lightly browned. Place large plate over skillet. Invert frittata onto plate. Return frittata, uncooked side down, to skillet. Cook about 4 minutes more or until center is just set. Cut into 6 wedges to serve.
*Makes 6 servings*

## SCRAMBLED EGGS WITH TAMALES

**1 can (15 ounces) tamales
8 eggs
2 tablespoons milk
½ teaspoon salt
2 tablespoons butter or margarine
1 large tomato, chopped
2 tablespoons minced onion
2 tablespoons diced green chilies
1 cup (4 ounces) shredded Monterey Jack
   cheese**

**1.** Preheat oven to 350°F.

**2.** Drain tamales, reserving ½ of sauce from can. Remove paper wrappings from tamales; place tamales in single layer in 10×6-inch baking dish. Cover with reserved sauce. Bake 10 minutes or until heated through.

**3.** Whisk eggs, milk and salt in medium bowl. Set aside.

**4.** Melt butter in large skillet over medium heat. Add tomato, onion and chilies. Cook 2 minutes or until vegetables are heated through. Add egg mixture. Cook, stirring gently, until eggs are soft set.

**5.** Remove tamales from oven. Spoon eggs over tamales; sprinkle with cheese. Broil 4 inches below heat 30 seconds or just until cheese melts.
*Makes 4 to 6 servings*

**Left to right:** *Greek Three Pepper Salad* (page 104)
*and Artichoke Frittata*

# — *Dazzling* —

# BREADS & COFFEE CAKES

## FRENCH RAISIN TOAST

**2 tablespoons sugar**
**1 teaspoon ground cinnamon**
**4 eggs, lightly beaten**
**½ cup milk**
**8 slices raisin bread**
**4 tablespoons butter or margarine, divided**
**Powdered sugar**

**1.** Combine sugar and cinnamon in wide shallow bowl. Beat in eggs and milk. Add bread; let stand to coat, then turn to coat other side.

**2.** Heat 2 tablespoons butter in large skillet over medium-low heat. Add bread slices; cook until brown. Turn and cook other side. Remove and keep warm. Repeat with remaining butter and bread. Sprinkle with powdered sugar.

*Makes 4 servings*

BREADS & COFFEE CAKES

# BLUEBERRY-CHEESE PANCAKES

2 cups all-purpose flour
2 teaspoons baking powder
¼ teaspoon baking soda
¼ teaspoon salt
2 tablespoons sugar
2 tablespoons wheat germ
1½ cups milk
1 cup cottage cheese, pressed through
   a sieve
1 egg, lightly beaten
¼ cup vegetable oil
1 cup fresh or frozen blueberries

**1.** Sift flour, baking powder, baking soda and salt into medium bowl. Stir in sugar and wheat germ; set aside.

**2.** Combine milk, cottage cheese, egg and oil in small bowl.

**3.** Pour liquid ingredients, all at once, into dry ingredients; stir until moistened. Add additional milk if batter is too thick; it should pour easily from spoon. Gently stir in blueberries.

**4.** Preheat griddle or large skillet over medium heat; grease lightly. Pour about ½ cup batter onto hot griddle for each pancake. Cook until tops of pancakes are bubbly and appear dry; turn and cook until lightly browned, about 2 minutes.

*Makes about 10 pancakes*

### *Keeping Pancakes Warm*

*You can keep pancakes warm until ready to serve by placing them on a plate or baking dish in a 200°F oven. Layer paper towels between pancakes to absorb steam and keep them from getting soggy.*

*Blueberry-Cheese Pancakes*

*BREADS & COFFEE CAKES*

# CHOCOLATE WAFFLES

 2 cups all-purpose flour
¼ cup unsweetened cocoa powder
 2 tablespoons sugar
 1 tablespoon baking powder
½ teaspoon salt
 2 cups milk
 2 eggs, beaten
¼ cup vegetable oil
 1 teaspoon vanilla extract
 Raspberry Syrup (recipe follows)

**1.** Preheat waffle iron; grease lightly.

**2.** Sift flour, cocoa, sugar, baking powder and salt into large bowl. Combine milk, eggs, oil and vanilla in small bowl. Stir liquid ingredients into dry ingredients until moistened.

**3.** For each waffle, pour about ¾ cup batter into waffle iron. Close lid and bake until steaming stops.* Serve with Raspberry Syrup.

*Makes about 6 waffles*

*Check manufacturer's directions for recommended amount of batter and baking time.

Raspberry Syrup
 1 cup water
 1 cup sugar
 1 package (10 ounces) frozen raspberries in
 syrup

**1.** Combine water and sugar in large saucepan. Cook over medium heat, stirring constantly, until sugar has dissolved. Continue cooking until mixture thickens slightly, about 10 minutes.

**2.** Stir in frozen raspberries; cook, stirring, until berries are thawed. Bring to a boil; continue cooking until syrup thickens slightly, about 5 to 10 minutes. Serve warm.    *Makes about 1⅓ cups*

*Chocolate Waffles with Raspberry Syrup*

**BREADS & COFFEE CAKES**

## STRAWBERRY & BANANA STUFFED FRENCH TOAST

    1 loaf (12 inches) French bread
    2 tablespoons strawberry jam
    4 ounces cream cheese, softened
    ¼ cup chopped strawberries
    ¼ cup chopped banana
    6 eggs, lightly beaten
    ¾ cup milk
    3 tablespoons butter or margarine, divided
      Strawberry Sauce (page 8)

**1.** Cut French bread into eight 1½-inch slices. Make pocket in each slice by cutting slit from top of bread almost to bottom.

**2.** Combine jam, cream cheese, strawberries and banana in small bowl to make filling.

**3.** Place heaping tablespoon of strawberry filling into each pocket. Press back together.

**4.** Beat eggs and milk in wide shallow bowl. Add bread; let stand to coat, then turn to coat other side.

**5.** Heat 2 tablespoons butter in large skillet over medium-low heat. Add as many bread slices as will fit; cook until brown. Turn and cook other side. Remove and keep warm. Repeat with remaining butter and bread slices. Serve with Strawberry Sauce.　　　　*Makes 8 slices*

*Here is a simple way to tell if the pan is hot enough to cook your eggs, pancakes or French toast. After heating the pan, flick a few drops of water onto it. If the pan is hot enough the water should skitter and dance around before evaporating. If the water does not hop around, continue heating the pan and try again. If the water evaporates immediately, the pan is too hot. Remove it from the heat for a minute or two to cool it off.*

**Top to bottom:** *Strawberry Sauce* (page 8) *and Strawberry & Banana Stuffed French Toast*

## PEAR BREAD PUDDING

**4 eggs, beaten**
**¾ cup sugar**
**3 cups milk**
**1 tablespoon vanilla extract**
**8 slices egg bread, crusts removed**
**3 to 4 tablespoons butter or margarine, softened**
**1 can (16 ounces) sliced pears, drained, sliced *or* 1 cup sliced cooked pears**
**Vanilla Sauce (recipe follows) or cream**

**1.** Grease 9×9-inch baking dish.

**2.** Combine eggs and sugar in large bowl. Gradually stir in milk and vanilla; set aside.

**3.** Lightly spread both sides of bread with butter. Arrange layer of bread slices in dish; top with another layer of bread slices. Arrange pear slices on bread. Pour egg mixture over bread and pears; let stand 30 minutes.

**4.** Preheat oven to 350°F. Place dish in larger pan, then fill larger pan with enough hot water to come halfway up sides of dish.

**5.** Bake about 55 minutes or until mixture is puffed and knife inserted near center comes out clean. Serve warm with Vanilla Sauce or cream.

*Makes 10 servings*

### Vanilla Sauce

**1 cup sugar**
**3 tablespoons all-purpose flour**
**3 tablespoons cornstarch**
**4½ cups milk**
**4 egg yolks, beaten**
**2 tablespoons butter or margarine**
**1 tablespoon vanilla extract**

**1.** Combine sugar, flour and cornstarch in large saucepan.

**2.** Gradually whisk in milk. Cook over medium heat, stirring constantly, until mixture comes to a boil, 10 to 15 minutes. Remove from heat.

**3.** Stir 1 cup of hot mixture into egg yolks. Stir egg yolk mixture into hot mixture; return to heat. Cook, stirring constantly, until mixture is bubbly. Continue cooking, stirring constantly, 2 minutes. Pour into heatproof bowl; stir in butter and cool. Stir in vanilla.

*Makes about 5 cups*

***Top to bottom:*** *Pear Bread Pudding and Blueberry Lattice Coffee Cake* (page 68)

**BREADS & COFFEE CAKES**

# BLUEBERRY LATTICE COFFEE CAKE

**1 package (¼ ounce) active dry yeast**
**1 teaspoon sugar**
**¼ cup warm water (110°F)**
**1 egg, beaten**
**½ cup butter or margarine, softened**
**⅓ cup milk**
**3 cups all-purpose flour**
**¼ cup sugar**
**½ teaspoon salt**
**2 packages (8 ounces each) cream cheese, softened**
**2 egg yolks**
**⅔ cup sugar**
**1 teaspoon vanilla extract or lemon extract**
**1 tablespoon grated lemon peel (optional)**
**1 cup fresh or frozen blueberries**

**1.** Dissolve yeast and 1 teaspoon sugar in warm water in large bowl. Let stand 10 minutes.

**2.** Beat in 1 egg, butter and milk. Beat in flour, ¼ cup sugar and salt to make soft dough. Knead on lightly floured surface about 10 minutes or until smooth and satiny, adding more flour as necessary to prevent sticking. Cover and let rest while making filling.

**3.** Combine cream cheese, 2 egg yolks, ⅔ cup sugar, vanilla and lemon peel in medium bowl. Beat until combined; set aside.

**4.** Grease 13×9-inch pan. Divide dough into thirds; set ⅓ aside. Roll out remaining ⅔ of dough to 13×9-inch rectangle. Place in greased pan and press dough ½ inch up sides to contain filling.

**5.** Spoon filling into dough-lined pan. Arrange blueberries over filling, pressing blueberries lightly into filling. Roll out remaining dough to 10-inch square. Cut dough into 1-inch strips. Arrange strips diagonally across pan in lattice pattern over filling, sealing strips to edges.

**6.** Cover with plastic wrap and refrigerate at least 2 hours or overnight.

**7.** Preheat oven to 350°F. Bake, uncovered, about 40 minutes or until lightly browned and filling is set. Serve warm or at room temperature.

*Makes 1 coffee cake (15 servings)*

BREADS & COFFEE CAKES

## STRAWBERRY MUFFINS

1¼ cups all-purpose flour
2½ teaspoons baking powder
½ teaspoon salt
1 cup rolled oats
½ cup sugar
1 cup milk
½ cup butter or margarine, melted
1 egg, beaten
1 teaspoon vanilla extract
1 cup chopped strawberries

**1.** Preheat oven to 425°F. Grease 12 (2½-inch) muffin cups.

**2.** Sift flour, baking powder and salt into large bowl. Stir in rolled oats and sugar; set aside. Combine milk, butter, egg and vanilla in small bowl. Stir milk mixture into dry ingredients just until moistened. Stir in strawberries.

**3.** Spoon batter into prepared muffin cups, filling each ⅔ full. Bake 15 to 18 minutes or until lightly browned and toothpick inserted in center comes out clean. *Makes 12 muffins*

## HAM & SWISS CHEESE BISCUITS

2 cups all-purpose flour
2 teaspoons baking powder
½ teaspoon baking soda
½ cup butter or margarine, chilled, cut into pieces
½ cup (2 ounces) shredded Swiss cheese
2 ounces ham, minced
About ⅔ cup buttermilk

**1.** Preheat oven to 450°F. Grease baking sheet.

**2.** Sift flour, baking powder and baking soda into medium bowl. Using pastry blender or 2 knives, cut in butter until mixture resembles coarse crumbs. Stir in cheese, ham and enough buttermilk to make soft dough.

**3.** Turn out dough onto lightly floured surface; knead lightly. Roll out dough ½ inch thick. Cut biscuit rounds with 2-inch cutter. Place on greased baking sheet.

**4.** Bake about 10 minutes or until browned.
*Makes about 18 biscuits*

# APPLE-ALMOND COFFEE CAKES

    1 package (¼ ounce) active dry yeast
    1 teaspoon sugar
    ¼ cup warm water (110°F)
    4 eggs, divided
    ½ cup butter or margarine, softened
    ⅓ cup milk
    3 cups all-purpose flour
    1¼ cups sugar, divided
    ½ teaspoon salt
    1½ packages (7 ounces each) almond paste
    4 small apples

**1.** Dissolve yeast and 1 teaspoon sugar in warm water in large bowl. Let stand 5 minutes or until mixture is bubbly. (If yeast does not bubble, it is no longer active and dough will not rise.)

**2.** Beat in 1 egg, butter and milk. Beat in flour, ¼ cup sugar and salt to make soft dough. Knead on lightly floured surface about 10 minutes or until smooth and satiny, adding flour as necessary to prevent sticking. Cover and let rest while making filling.

**3.** Cut almond paste into small pieces. Combine almond paste, remaining 3 eggs and ¾ cup sugar in blender or food processor. Cover; process until combined. Set aside.

**4.** Grease two 9-inch round cake pans. Divide dough in half. Roll out ½ of dough to 9-inch circle. Place in greased pan and press dough ½ inch up side to contain filling. Repeat with remaining dough.

**5.** Divide almond filling equally between pans. Cover with plastic wrap and refrigerate at least 2 hours or overnight.

**6.** Preheat oven to 350°F. Core apples and cut into thin slices; do not peel. Arrange apple slices over almond filling. Sprinkle each coffee cake with 2 tablespoons sugar. Bake 40 to 50 minutes or until filling is set. Serve warm or at room temperature.

*Makes 2 coffee cakes (8 to 10 servings each)*

*Top to bottom: Strawberry Muffins* (page 69)
*and Apple-Almond Coffee Cake*

## BREADS & COFFEE CAKES

## CARAMEL-TOPPED MEGA MUFFINS

 1 cup raisin and bran cereal
 ¾ cup milk
 ¼ cup unprocessed wheat bran
 ¾ cup molasses
 ¼ cup vegetable oil
 1 egg, beaten
 2 cups all-purpose flour
 1 tablespoon baking powder
 2 teaspoons ground cinnamon
 ½ teaspoon baking soda
 ½ teaspoon salt
 ½ cup raisins (optional)
 3 tablespoons butter or margarine
 3 tablespoons packed brown sugar
 2 tablespoons light corn syrup

**1.** Preheat oven to 350°F. Grease 6 large (4-inch) muffin cups.

**2.** Combine cereal, milk and wheat bran in medium bowl. Let stand about 10 minutes to soften. Stir in molasses, oil and egg. Sift flour, baking powder, cinnamon, baking soda and salt into large bowl. Stir liquid ingredients into dry ingredients just until combined. Stir in raisins.

**3.** Fill muffin cups, using about ½ cup batter for each muffin. Bake 28 to 30 minutes or until toothpick inserted in center comes out clean. Immediately turn out onto cooling rack.

**4.** Combine butter, brown sugar and corn syrup in small saucepan over medium heat. Cook, stirring constantly, until sugar has dissolved. Bring to a boil. Cook, stirring constantly, 3 to 4 minutes or until thickened. Pour 1 tablespoon of mixture over each muffin. *Makes 6 large muffins*

## ROASTED RED PEPPER BISCUITS

 2 cups buttermilk biscuit mix
 ½ cup PROGRESSO® Grated Parmesan
   Cheese
 1 teaspoon dried oregano leaves
 ⅛ teaspoon cayenne pepper
 1 jar (7 ounces) PROGRESSO® Roasted
   Peppers (red), drained, patted dry on
   paper towel and chopped
 ⅔ cup milk

**1.** Preheat oven to 425°F.

**2.** In medium bowl, stir together biscuit mix, Parmesan cheese, oregano and cayenne pepper.

**3.** Add roasted peppers and milk to biscuit mixture; stir just until moistened.

**4.** Drop dough by heaping tablespoonfuls, 2 inches apart, onto greased baking sheet.

**5.** Bake 12 to 14 minutes or until browned.

*Makes 1 dozen*

*Roasted Red Pepper Biscuits*

## SOUR CREAM COFFEE CAKE WITH BRANDY-SOAKED CHERRIES

 Streusel Topping (recipe follows)
3¼ **cups all-purpose flour, divided**
 1 **cup dry sweet or sour cherries**
 ½ **cup brandy**
1½ **cups sugar**
 ¾ **cup butter or margarine**
 3 **eggs**
 1 **container (16 ounces) sour cream**
 1 **tablespoon vanilla**
 2 **teaspoons baking powder**
 2 **teaspoons baking soda**
 ¼ **teaspoon salt**

**1.** Prepare Streusel Topping; set aside.

**2.** Preheat oven to 350°F. Grease 10-inch tube pan with removable bottom. Sprinkle ¼ cup flour into pan, rotating pan to evenly coat bottom and sides of pan. Discard any remaining flour.

**3.** Bring cherries and brandy to a boil in small saucepan over high heat. When mixture comes to a boil, cover and remove from heat. Let stand 20 to 30 minutes or until cherries are tender. Drain; discard any remaining brandy.

**4.** Beat sugar and butter in large bowl with electric mixer at medium speed until light and fluffy, scraping down side of bowl once. Add eggs, 1 at a time, beating until thoroughly incorporated. Beat in sour cream and vanilla.

**5.** Add remaining 3 cups flour, baking powder, baking soda and salt. Beat with electric mixer at low speed just until blended. Stir in cherries.

**6.** Spoon ½ of batter into prepared tube pan. Sprinkle with ½ of Streusel Topping. Repeat with remaining batter and Streusel Topping. Bake 1 hour or until wooden skewer inserted into center comes out clean.

**7.** Cool in pan on wire rack 10 minutes. Remove from pan. Serve warm or at room temperature. Garnish as desired. *Makes 16 servings*

### Streusel Topping

 1 **cup chopped walnuts or pecans**
 ½ **cup packed brown sugar**
 1 **teaspoon ground cinnamon**
 ½ **teaspoon ground nutmeg**
 2 **tablespoons melted butter or margarine**

**1.** Combine nuts, brown sugar, cinnamon and nutmeg in small bowl.

**2.** Drizzle mixture with butter and toss with fork until evenly mixed.

*Sour Cream Coffee Cake with Brandy-Soaked Cherries*

BREADS & COFFEE CAKES

# APRICOT RING

**FILLING**
 1 cup dried apricots, chopped
 1 cup apple juice
 ¾ cup sugar or to taste

**DOUGH**
 1 package (¼ ounce) active dry yeast
 4 tablespoons sugar, divided
 1 cup warm water (110°F)
 About 4 cups all-purpose flour, divided
 1 teaspoon salt
 2 eggs, beaten
 ¼ cup butter or margarine, softened
 1 egg white, lightly beaten
 2 tablespoons sliced almonds

**1.** To make filling, combine apricots and apple juice in small saucepan over medium heat. Cover and cook, stirring occasionally, about 12 minutes or until apricots are tender and juice is absorbed. Stir in sugar to taste. Cook, stirring constantly, about 3 minutes or until mixture is thick paste. Cool.

**2.** To make dough, dissolve yeast and 1 tablespoon sugar in warm water in large bowl of electric mixer. Let stand 10 minutes. Add remaining 3 tablespoons sugar, 1 cup flour and salt.

**3.** Beat with electric mixer 2 minutes. Add 2 eggs and butter. Beat 1 minute. Stir in enough of remaining 3 cups flour to make soft dough.

**4.** Knead dough on lightly floured surface about 10 minutes or until smooth, adding flour as necessary to prevent sticking. Cover and let rest 20 minutes.

**5.** Grease large baking sheet. On lightly floured surface, roll dough to 18×11-inch rectangle. Spread filling over dough. Roll up jelly-roll style, starting at long side. Seal edge; form into ring on greased baking sheet, sealing ends.

**6.** Cut ring at 1-inch intervals about two-thirds of the way through, using kitchen scissors or sharp knife. Turn each slice outward to form a petal as you cut.

**7.** Cover with damp cloth and let rise in warm place until doubled in bulk, about 45 minutes.

**8.** Preheat oven to 350°F. Brush with egg white and sprinkle with almonds. Bake about 30 minutes or until browned.

*Makes 1 large coffee cake (15 to 18 servings)*

BREADS & COFFEE CAKES

## ANGEL BISCUITS

⅓ cup warm water (110°F)
1 package (¼ ounce) active dry yeast
5 cups all-purpose flour
3 tablespoons sugar
1 tablespoon baking powder
1 teaspoon baking soda
1 teaspoon salt
1 cup shortening
2 cups buttermilk

**1.** Preheat oven to 450°F. Pour warm water into small bowl. Sprinkle yeast over water and stir until dissolved. Let stand 10 minutes or until small bubbles form.

**2.** Combine flour, sugar, baking powder, baking soda and salt in large bowl. Add shortening. With fingers, pastry blender or 2 knives, rub or cut in shortening until mixture resembles fine crumbs. Make a well in center. Pour in yeast mixture and buttermilk; stir with fork until mixture forms dough.

**3.** Turn dough out onto lightly floured board. Knead 30 seconds or until dough feels light and soft but not sticky. Roll out desired amount of dough to ½-inch thickness. Cut biscuit rounds with 2-inch cutter. Place biscuits close together (for soft sides) or ½ inch apart (for crispy sides) on ungreased baking sheet. Bake 15 to 18 minutes or until tops are lightly browned.

**4.** Place remaining dough in resealable food storage bag; refrigerate up to 3 days. Or, roll out and cut remaining dough into rounds; place on baking sheet and freeze. Transfer frozen rounds to resealable food storage bags; return to freezer. At baking time, place frozen rounds on ungreased baking sheet. Let stand 20 minutes or until thawed before baking. Bake as directed.

*Makes about 5 dozen biscuits*

## BLUE CORN MUFFINS

1 cup all-purpose flour
¾ cup blue cornmeal
2 tablespoons sugar
1½ teaspoons baking powder
½ teaspoon baking soda
¼ teaspoon salt
2 eggs
1 cup buttermilk or sour cream
¼ cup butter or margarine, melted
Honey Butter (recipe page 82)

Preheat oven to 400°F. Grease 12 (2½-inch) muffin cups. Combine flour, cornmeal, sugar, baking powder, baking soda and salt in large bowl. Beat eggs, buttermilk and butter in small bowl until blended. Pour liquid mixture into dry ingredients; stir just until moistened. Fill each prepared muffin cup ⅔ full with batter. Bake 15 to 20 minutes or until a wooden pick inserted in centers comes out clean. Remove muffins from pan to wire rack; cool 5 minutes. Meanwhile, prepare Honey Butter; serve with warm muffins.

*Makes 12 muffins*

# BREADS & COFFEE CAKES

## SPICY SWEET POTATO MUFFINS

   2 tablespoons packed brown sugar
   2 teaspoons ground cinnamon, divided
1½ cups all-purpose flour
   2 teaspoons baking powder
  ½ teaspoon salt
  ½ teaspoon baking soda
  ½ teaspoon ground allspice
  ⅓ cup packed brown sugar
   1 cup mashed cooked or canned sweet
      potatoes
  ¾ cup buttermilk
  ¼ cup vegetable oil
   1 egg, beaten

**1.** Preheat oven to 425°F. Grease 12 (2½-inch) muffin cups.

**2.** Combine 2 tablespoons brown sugar and 1 teaspoon cinnamon in small bowl; set aside.

**3.** Sift flour, baking powder, remaining 1 teaspoon cinnamon, salt, baking soda and allspice into large bowl. Stir in ⅓ cup brown sugar.

**4.** In medium bowl, combine sweet potatoes, buttermilk, oil and egg. Stir buttermilk mixture into dry ingredients just until combined. Spoon batter into prepared muffin cups, filling each ⅔ full. Sprinkle each muffin with ½ teaspoon of cinnamon mixture. Bake about 14 to 16 minutes or until toothpick inserted in center comes out clean.

*Makes 12 muffins*

## MUFFIN SURPRISE

1½ cups all-purpose flour
2½ teaspoons baking powder
  ¼ teaspoon salt
   1 cup oat bran
  ½ cup packed light brown sugar
   1 cup milk
  ⅓ cup vegetable oil
   2 eggs, lightly beaten
   1 teaspoon vanilla extract
   1 package (3 ounces) cream cheese
  ¾ cup apricot-pineapple jam

**1.** Preheat oven to 425°F. Grease 12 (2½-inch) muffin cups.

**2.** Sift flour, baking powder and salt into large bowl. Stir in oat bran and brown sugar; set aside. In small bowl, combine milk, oil, eggs and vanilla. Stir milk mixture into dry ingredients just until moistened.

**3.** Cut cream cheese into 12 equal pieces. Spoon about ½ of batter into prepared muffin cups, filling about ⅓ full. Spoon about 1 tablespoon jam on top of batter. Top with 1 piece of cream cheese. Spoon remaining batter over jam and cheese, filling each muffin cup ⅔ full. Bake about 14 to 16 minutes or until browned. *Makes 12 muffins*

**Top to bottom:** *Spicy Sweet Potato Muffins and Muffin Surprise*

# PECAN STICKY BUNS

**DOUGH***
  4 to 5 cups flour, divided
  ½ cup granulated sugar
 1½ teaspoons salt
  2 packages active dry yeast
  ¾ cup warm milk (105° to 115°F)
  ½ cup warm water (105° to 115°F)
  ¼ cup (½ stick) MAZOLA® margarine or
     butter, softened
  2 eggs

**GLAZE**
  ½ cup KARO® Dark or Light Corn Syrup
  ½ cup packed light brown sugar
  ¼ cup (½ stick) MAZOLA® margarine or
     butter
  1 cup pecans, coarsely chopped

**FILLING**
  ½ cup packed light brown sugar
  1 teaspoon cinnamon
  2 tablespoons MAZOLA® margarine or
     butter, melted

**For Dough*:** In large bowl combine 2 cups flour, sugar, salt and yeast. Stir in milk, water and softened margarine until blended. Stir in eggs and enough additional flour (about 2 cups) to make a soft dough. Knead on floured surface until smooth and elastic, about 8 minutes. Cover dough and let rest on floured surface 10 minutes.

**For Glaze:** Meanwhile, in small saucepan over low heat stir corn syrup, brown sugar and margarine until smooth. Pour into 13×9×2-inch baking pan. Sprinkle with pecans; set aside.

**For Filling:** Combine brown sugar and cinnamon; set aside. Roll dough to a 20×12-inch rectangle. Brush dough with 2 tablespoons melted margarine; sprinkle with brown sugar mixture. Starting from a long side, roll up jelly-roll fashion. Pinch seam to seal. Cut into 15 slices; place cut-side up in prepared pan. Cover tightly. Refrigerate 2 to 24 hours.

To bake, preheat oven to 375°F. Remove pan from refrigerator; uncover and let stand at room temperature 10 minutes. Bake 28 to 30 minutes or until tops are browned. Invert onto serving tray. Serve warm or cool completely.   *Makes 15 buns*

**Prep Time:** 30 minutes, plus chilling
**Bake Time:** 28 minutes

**\*TO USE FROZEN BREAD DOUGH:** Thaw 2 loaves (1 lb. each) frozen bread dough in refrigerator overnight. Press loaves together and roll into a 20×12-inch rectangle; complete as recipe directs.

*Pecan Sticky Buns*

BREADS & COFFEE CAKES

## LEMON YOGURT COFFEE CAKE

⅓ cup canola oil
⅔ cup honey
1 egg
¾ cup cholesterol-free egg substitute
1½ teaspoons lemon extract
1¾ cups all-purpose flour
¾ cup whole wheat pastry flour or whole wheat flour
2½ teaspoons baking powder
1 cup DANNON® Lemon Lowfat Yogurt
1 tablespoon grated lemon peel
1 cup coarsely chopped cranberries

Preheat oven to 350°F. Grease and flour a 9-cup kugelhopf or 9-inch bundt pan. In a large bowl beat oil and honey until creamy. Add egg, egg substitute and lemon extract; beat until blended. In a medium bowl combine flours and baking powder; stir into honey mixture alternately with yogurt. Fold in lemon peel and cranberries. Pour into prepared pan; smooth top.

Bake 30 to 35 minutes or until toothpick inserted into center comes out clean. Cool in pan on wire rack. To serve, invert coffee cake onto platter or cake plate.           *12 to 16 servings*

## CROISSANT TOAST

4 eggs, lightly beaten
¾ cup milk
2 tablespoons brandy (optional)
1 tablespoon sugar
2 teaspoons vanilla extract
4 day-old croissants, halved horizontally
4 tablespoons butter or margarine, divided

**1.** Beat eggs, milk, brandy, sugar and vanilla in wide shallow bowl. Add croissants, cut-side down; let stand to coat, then turn to coat other side.

**2.** Heat 2 tablespoons butter in large skillet over medium-low heat. Add croissant halves; cook until brown. Turn and cook other side. Remove and keep warm. Repeat with remaining butter and croissants. Serve warm with maple syrup.

*Makes 4 servings*

---

### *Honey Butter*

*For a sweet spread that is terrific on everything from muffins to toast, combine equal amounts of softened butter or margarine and honey, then add a little vanilla extract. You'll want to keep a batch of this on hand to sweeten all your breakfasts.*

---

*Lemon Yogurt Coffee Cake*

## CHOCOLATE CHUNK SOUR CREAM MUFFINS

1½ **cups all-purpose flour**
½ **cup sugar**
1½ **teaspoons CALUMET® Baking Powder**
½ **teaspoon cinnamon**
¼ **teaspoon salt**
2 **eggs, lightly beaten**
½ **cup milk**
½ **cup sour cream or plain yogurt**
¼ **cup (½ stick) margarine, melted**
1 **teaspoon vanilla**
1 **package (4 ounces) BAKER'S®**
   **GERMAN'S® Sweet Chocolate, chopped**

**HEAT** oven to 375°F.

**MIX** flour, sugar, baking powder, cinnamon and salt; set aside. Stir eggs, milk, sour cream, margarine and vanilla in large bowl until well blended. Add flour mixture; stir until just moistened. Stir in chocolate.

**FILL** 12 paper- or foil-lined muffin cups ⅔ full with batter.

**BAKE** for 30 minutes or until toothpick inserted into center comes out clean. Remove from pan to cool on wire rack.          *Makes 12 muffins*

**Prep time:** 15 minutes
**Baking time:** 30 minutes

## CHOCOLATE CHUNK BANANA BREAD

2 **eggs, lightly beaten**
1 **cup mashed ripe bananas (about**
   **3 medium bananas)**
⅓ **cup vegetable oil**
¼ **cup milk**
2 **cups all-purpose flour**
1 **cup sugar**
2 **teaspoons CALUMET® Baking Powder**
¼ **teaspoon salt**
1 **package (4 ounces) BAKER'S®**
   **GERMAN'S® Sweet Chocolate, coarsely**
   **chopped**
½ **cup chopped nuts**

**HEAT** oven to 350°F.

**STIR** eggs, bananas, oil and milk until well blended. Add flour, sugar, baking powder and salt; stir until just moistened. Stir in chocolate and nuts. Pour into greased 9×5-inch loaf pan.

**BAKE** for 55 minutes or until toothpick inserted into center comes out clean. Cool in pan 10 minutes. Remove from pan to cool on wire rack.
*Makes 1 loaf*

**Prep time:** 20 minutes
**Baking time:** 55 minutes

*Chocolate Chunk Sour Cream Muffins and*
*Chocolate Chunk Banana Bread*

BREADS & COFFEE CAKES

## ORANGE FRENCH TOAST

**1 cup fresh orange juice**
**2 tablespoons grated orange peel**
**1 tablespoon frozen orange juice**
    **concentrate, thawed**
**5 eggs**
**2 tablespoons granulated sugar**
**½ cup DANNON® Plain Nonfat or Lowfat**
    **Yogurt**
**1 loaf braided bread or brioche bread**
**1 tablespoon butter or margarine**
    **Confectioner's sugar**
    **Orange slices**

In a large bowl combine orange juice, orange peel, orange juice concentrate, eggs and granulated sugar. Beat until well blended. Stir in yogurt. Cut bread into 1- to 1½-inch-thick slices (about 16 slices). Dip bread slices into egg mixture, turning to coat. Place in single layer in a shallow pan. Pour any remaining egg mixture over slices. Cover; chill up to 2 hours.

Heat griddle or large skillet over medium-high heat. Melt butter in pan. Lightly brown French toast on both sides. Keep French toast warm in oven until ready to serve. Dust with confectioner's sugar and garnish with orange slices before serving.

*8 servings*

## RAISIN OAT SCONES

**2 cups all-purpose flour**
**2 teaspoons baking powder**
**½ teaspoon baking soda**
**¼ teaspoon salt**
**1 cup rolled oats**
**½ cup butter or margarine, chilled, cut into**
    **pieces**
**1 cup raisins**
    **About 1 cup buttermilk**

**1.** Preheat oven to 425°F. Grease baking sheet.

**2.** Sift flour, baking powder, baking soda and salt into medium bowl. Stir in oats. Using pastry blender or 2 knives, cut in butter until mixture resembles coarse crumbs. Add raisins. Stir in enough buttermilk to make soft dough.

**3.** Turn out dough onto lightly floured surface; knead until smooth. Roll out dough to 12×10-inch rectangle. Cut into 2-inch squares.

**4.** Arrange scones on prepared baking sheet. Bake about 15 minutes or until browned.

*Makes 30 scones*

*Orange French Toast*

# — *Elegant* —

## BRUNCH DISHES

### SPARKLING WHITE SANGRIA

1 cup KARO® Light Corn Syrup
1 orange, sliced
1 lemon, sliced
1 lime, sliced
½ cup orange-flavored liqueur
1 bottle (750 ml) dry white wine
2 tablespoons lemon juice
1 bottle (12 ounces) club soda or seltzer,
   chilled
Additional fresh fruit (optional)

In large pitcher combine corn syrup, orange, lemon and lime slices and liqueur. Let stand 20 to 30 minutes, stirring occasionally. Stir in wine and lemon juice. Refrigerate. Just before serving, add soda and ice cubes. If desired, garnish with additional fruit.

*Makes about 6 (8-oz.) servings*

**Prep Time:** 15 minutes, plus standing and chilling

# BRUNCH DISHES

## BROCCOLI-SALMON QUICHE

1 (9-inch) Pastry Shell (recipe follows)
1 tablespoon vegetable oil
1½ cups chopped broccoli
⅓ cup chopped onion
⅓ cup chopped red bell pepper
½ cup (2 ounces) shredded Swiss cheese
1 cup flaked canned or cooked salmon
    (about 5 ounces)
3 eggs, beaten
1¼ cups milk
1 teaspoon dried tarragon leaves
¼ teaspoon salt
⅛ teaspoon freshly ground pepper

**1.** Preheat oven to 425°F.

**2.** Place piece of foil inside pastry shell; partially fill with uncooked beans or rice. Bake 10 minutes. Remove foil and beans; continue baking 5 minutes or until lightly browned. Let cool.

**3.** *Reduce oven temperature to 375°F.*

**4.** Heat oil in medium skillet over medium heat. Add broccoli, onion and bell pepper; cook and stir 3 to 4 minutes or until crisp-tender. Set aside to cool.

**5.** Sprinkle cheese over bottom of pastry shell. Arrange salmon and vegetables over cheese.

**6.** Combine eggs, milk, tarragon, salt and pepper in medium bowl. Pour over salmon and vegetables.

**7.** Bake 35 to 40 minutes or until filling is puffed and knife inserted in center comes out clean. Let stand 10 minutes before cutting.

*Makes 6 servings*

Pastry Shell
1½ cups all-purpose flour
¼ teaspoon salt
¼ cup butter or margarine, chilled
¼ cup shortening
4 to 5 tablespoons cold water

**1.** Combine flour and salt in large bowl. With pastry blender or 2 knives, cut in butter and shortening until mixture resembles cornmeal.

**2.** Add water, 1 tablespoon at a time; stir just until mixture holds together. Knead lightly with your hands to form ball. Wrap in plastic wrap and refrigerate 30 minutes.

**3.** Roll out dough on lightly floured surface to 12-inch circle. Gently press into 9-inch quiche dish or pie pan. Trim edges and flute.

*Broccoli-Salmon Quiche*

## FETA BRUNCH BAKE

    1 medium red bell pepper
    2 bags (10 ounces each) fresh spinach
    6 eggs
    6 ounces crumbled feta cheese
    ⅓ cup chopped onion
    2 tablespoons chopped fresh parsley
    ¼ teaspoon dried dill weed
      Dash black pepper

**1.** Cover broiler pan with aluminum foil. Set broiler pan about 4 inches from heat. Preheat broiler. Place bell pepper on aluminum foil. Broil 15 to 20 minutes until blackened on all sides, turning every 5 minutes with tongs.

**2.** Place blackened bell pepper in paper bag. Close bag; set aside to cool 15 to 20 minutes.

**3.** Cut bell pepper in half; place pepper halves on cutting board. Peel off skin with paring knife; rinse under cold water to remove seeds. Cut bell pepper into ½-inch pieces.

**4.** Separate spinach into leaves and wash in cold water. Pat dry with paper towels.

**5.** Remove and discard stems from spinach leaves.

**6.** Heat 1 quart water in 2-quart saucepan over high heat to a boil. Add spinach. Return to a boil; boil 2 to 3 minutes until crisp-tender. Drain spinach from saucepan, then immediately plunge into cold water.

**7.** Drain spinach; let stand until cool enough to handle. Squeeze spinach between hands to remove excess water. Finely chop with chef's knife.

**8.** Preheat oven to 400°F. Grease 1-quart baking dish.

**9.** Beat eggs in large bowl with electric mixer at medium speed until frothy. Stir in bell pepper, spinach, cheese, onion, parsley, dill weed and black pepper.

**10.** Pour egg mixture into prepared dish. Bake 20 minutes or until set. Let stand 5 minutes before serving. Garnish as desired. *Makes 4 servings*

*Feta Brunch Bake*

# BRUNCH DISHES

## CHICKEN WITH MUSHROOM SAUCE

**MUSHROOM SAUCE**
   **3 tablespoons butter or margarine**
   **8 ounces fresh mushrooms, sliced**
   **3 tablespoons all-purpose flour**
**1½ cups chicken broth**
   **1 tablespoon minced chives**
   **1 tablespoon minced parsley**
   **1 teaspoon Dijon-style mustard**
   **¼ teaspoon salt**
   **⅛ teaspoon freshly ground pepper**
   **½ cup sour cream**

**CHICKEN**
   **1 tablespoon vegetable oil**
   **4 boneless skinless chicken breast halves**
   **4 slices ham**
   **4 slices Monterey Jack cheese**
   **2 English muffins, split and toasted**
   **½ red bell pepper, cut into thin strips**

**1.** For mushroom sauce, melt butter in medium saucepan over medium heat. Add mushrooms; cook until tender. Remove with slotted spoon; set aside. Stir flour into pan; cook until bubbly. Slowly whisk in broth.

**2.** Add mushrooms, chives, parsley, mustard, salt and pepper. Cook, stirring constantly, until thickened. Stir in sour cream; heat until hot. *Do not boil.* Keep warm on very low heat.

**3.** For chicken, heat oil in large skillet over medium heat. Add chicken; cook, turning occasionally, about 8 minutes or until chicken is browned and no longer pink in center.

**4.** Reduce heat to low; place ham, then cheese on chicken. Cover and cook 1 to 2 minutes or just until cheese melts. Place chicken on English muffins. Spoon sauce over chicken and top with pepper strips. *Makes 4 servings*

*A combination of melons (honeydew, watermelon, cantaloupe or any of the regional varieties) cut into different shapes makes a charming accompaniment to many brunch dishes. For a distinctive touch, top each serving with a splash of champagne.*

*Chicken with Mushroom Sauce*

## BRUNCH DISHES

## SEAFOOD SALAD SANDWICHES

**1 envelope LIPTON® Recipe Secrets®
  Vegetable Soup Mix**
**¾ cup sour cream**
**½ cup chopped celery**
**¼ cup mayonnaise**
**1 tablespoon fresh or frozen chopped
  chives (optional)**
**1 teaspoon lemon juice
  Hot pepper sauce to taste**
**⅛ teaspoon black pepper**
**2 packages (6 ounces each) frozen
  crabmeat, thawed and well drained\***
**4 hard rolls, split
  Lettuce leaves**

In large bowl, blend Vegetable Soup Mix, sour cream, celery, mayonnaise, chives, lemon juice, hot pepper sauce and black pepper. Stir in crabmeat; cover and refrigerate. To serve, line rolls with lettuce and fill with crab mixture.

*Makes 4 sandwiches*

**\*VARIATIONS:** Use 1 package (12 ounces) frozen cleaned shrimp, cooked and coarsely chopped; *or* 2 packages (8 ounces each) sea legs, thawed, drained and chopped *or* 1 can (13 ounces) tuna, drained and flaked; *or* 2 cans (4½ ounces each) medium or large shrimp, drained and chopped; *or* 2 cans (6½ ounces each) crabmeat, drained and flaked.

## MAKE-AHEAD BRUNCH BAKE

**1 pound bulk pork sausage**
**6 eggs, beaten**
**2 cups light cream or half-and-half**
**½ teaspoon salt**
**1 teaspoon ground mustard**
**1 cup (4 ounces) shredded Cheddar cheese**
**1 can (2.8 ounces) FRENCH'S® French Fried
  Onions**

Crumble sausage into large skillet. Cook over medium-high heat until browned; drain well. Stir in eggs, cream, salt, mustard, *½ cup* cheese and *½ can* French Fried Onions; mix well. Pour into greased 8×12-inch baking dish. Refrigerate, covered, 8 hours or overnight. Bake, uncovered, at 350° for 45 minutes or until knife inserted in center comes out clean. Top with remaining cheese and onions; bake, uncovered, 5 minutes or until onions are golden brown. Let stand 15 minutes before serving. *Makes 6 servings*

**MICROWAVE DIRECTIONS:** Crumble sausage into 8×12-inch microwave-safe dish. Cook, covered, on HIGH 4 to 6 minutes or until sausage is cooked. Stir sausage halfway through cooking time. Drain well. Stir in ingredients and refrigerate as above. Cook, covered, 10 to 15 minutes or until center is firm. Stir egg mixture halfway through cooking time. Top with remaining cheese and onions; cook, uncovered, 1 minute or until cheese melts. Let stand 5 minutes.

*Seafood Salad Sandwiches*

# BRUNCH DISHES

## HAM-EGG-BRIE STRUDEL

  4 eggs
  1 tablespoon minced green onion
  1 tablespoon minced parsley
  ¼ teaspoon salt
  ⅛ teaspoon freshly ground pepper
  1 tablespoon vegetable oil
  4 sheets phyllo pastry
  2 tablespoons butter or margarine, melted
  3 ounces sliced ham
  3 ounces Brie

**1.** Preheat oven to 375°F.

**2.** Lightly beat eggs; add onion, parsley, salt and pepper. Heat oil in medium skillet over medium-low heat. Add egg mixture. Cook and stir until softly scrambled. Set aside.

**3.** Place 1 phyllo sheet on large piece of waxed paper. Brush lightly with butter. Top with second phyllo sheet; brush with butter. Repeat with remaining phyllo. Arrange ½ of ham slices near short end of pastry, leaving 2-inch border around short end and sides. Place scrambled eggs on ham. Cut Brie into small pieces. Place over eggs. Top with remaining ham.

**4.** Fold long sides of phyllo in. Fold short end over ham. Use waxed paper to roll pastry to enclose filling. Place on lightly greased baking sheet, seam-side down. Brush with remaining butter. Bake about 15 minutes or until lightly browned.

*Makes 4 servings*

## ENDIVE-TOMATO SALAD

  ¼ cup olive oil
  1 tablespoon rice vinegar
  1 tablespoon balsamic vinegar *or* white
    wine vinegar
  1 tablespoon water
  2 tomatoes, thinly sliced
  2 teaspoons chopped fresh basil *or*
    ¾ teaspoon dried basil leaves
  2 teaspoons chopped fresh parsley
  1 head Belgian endive, separated into
    leaves

**1.** To prepare dressing, combine oil, vinegars and water in small bowl. Whisk until thickened; set aside.

**2.** Arrange tomatoes in center of round platter. Sprinkle with basil and parsley. Tuck endive leaves under tomato slices, arranging like spokes in a wheel. Drizzle dressing over salad.

*Makes 4 servings*

***Top to bottom:** Endive-Tomato Salad and
Ham-Egg-Brie Strudel*

## BRUNCH DISHES

## SPARKLING APPLE PUNCH

**2 bottles (750ml each) sparkling apple cider, chilled**
**1½ quarts papaya or apricot nectar, chilled**
**Ice**
**1 or 2 papayas, peeled and chopped**
**Orange slices, quartered**

Combine apple cider, papaya nectar and ice in punch bowl. Add papayas and orange slices.

*Makes about 4 quarts*

---

### Papaya

*Papaya is a tropical fruit with a flavor similar to melon. It is available year-round. You can tell the fruit is ripe when at least half the skin has turned yellow.*

---

## STRAWBERRY-PEACH COOLER

**1 cup sliced strawberries**
**1 cup chopped peaches**
**2 tablespoons sugar**
**1 bottle (750ml) white wine, chilled**
**1 bottle (1 quart) sparkling water, chilled**
**Mint sprigs**
**Ice**

**1.** Combine strawberries and peaches in small bowl. Sprinkle with sugar; stir gently. Let stand at room temperature 30 minutes.

**2.** Pour fruit into punch bowl. Gently pour in wine and water. Add mint sprigs and ice.

*Makes about 2 quarts*

**NONALCOHOLIC COOLER:** Use only 1 tablespoon sugar. Substitute 1 quart apple juice for wine.

*Left to right: Sparkling Apple Punch and Strawberry-Peach Cooler*

## BRUNCH DISHES

## HOLLANDAISE SAUCE

¾ cup HELLMANN'S® or BEST FOODS® Real or Light Mayonnaise or Reduced Fat Cholesterol Free Mayonnaise Dressing
⅓ cup milk
¼ teaspoon salt
   Dash freshly ground pepper
1 teaspoon grated lemon peel
1 tablespoon lemon juice

In small saucepan combine mayonnaise, milk, salt and pepper until smooth. Stirring constantly, cook over low heat about 3 minutes or just until heated. Stir in lemon peel and lemon juice. Serve with cooked asparagus, broccoli or other vegetables.

*Makes about 1 cup*

## SAUSAGE & APPLE QUICHE

1 (9-inch) Pastry Shell (page 90)
½ pound bulk spicy pork sausage
½ cup chopped onion
¾ cup shredded, peeled tart apple
1 tablespoon sugar
1 tablespoon lemon juice
⅛ teaspoon crushed red pepper flakes
1 cup (4 ounces) shredded Cheddar cheese
3 eggs
1½ cups half-and-half
¼ teaspoon salt
   Ground black pepper

**1.** Preheat oven to 425°F.

**2.** Place piece of foil inside pastry shell; partially fill with uncooked beans or rice. Bake 10 minutes. Remove foil and beans; continue baking pastry 5 minutes or until lightly browned. Let cool.

**3.** *Reduce oven temperature to 375°F.*

**4.** Crumble sausage into large skillet; add onion. Cook over medium heat until meat is browned and onion is tender. Spoon off and discard pan drippings.

**5.** Add apple, sugar, lemon juice and crushed red pepper to skillet. Cook on medium-high, stirring constantly, 4 minutes or until apple is just tender and all liquid is evaporated. Let cool.

**6.** Spoon sausage mixture into pastry shell; top with cheese. Whisk eggs, half-and-half, salt and dash of black pepper in medium bowl. Pour over cheese.

**7.** Bake 35 to 45 minutes or until filling is puffed and knife inserted in center comes out clean. Let stand 10 minutes before cutting.

*Makes 6 servings*

*Hollandaise Sauce*

## BRUNCH DISHES

## GREEK THREE PEPPER SALAD

**½ cup olive oil**
**2 tablespoons lemon juice**
**1 tablespoon water**
**2 teaspoons white wine vinegar**
**1 tablespoon chopped fresh parsley**
**¾ teaspoon minced fresh oregano** *or*
    **¼ teaspoon dried oregano leaves**
**½ teaspoon sugar**
**1 red bell pepper, thinly sliced**
**1 green bell pepper, thinly sliced**
**1 yellow or orange bell pepper, thinly sliced**
**½ red onion, thinly sliced**
**½ cup Greek-style olives**
**2 ounces feta cheese, crumbled**
  **Salt and pepper to taste**

**1.** Pour oil into small bowl. Add lemon juice, water, vinegar, parsley, oregano and sugar; whisk until thickened.

**2.** Combine bell peppers, onion and olives in large bowl. Add dressing. Toss to combine, cover and let stand at room temperature 1 hour. Drain off excess dressing. Add cheese to bell pepper mixture; toss. Season with salt and pepper.   *Makes 6 servings*

## HAM & CHEESE QUESADILLAS

**½ cup (2 ounces) shredded Monterey Jack cheese**
**½ cup (2 ounces) shredded Cheddar cheese**
**4 (10-inch) flour tortillas**
**4 ounces ham, finely chopped**
**¼ cup chopped canned green chilies**
  **Salsa (optional)**

**1.** Combine cheeses; divide equally between 2 tortillas. Place ham and green chilies over cheese. Top each with another tortilla.

**2.** Heat large skillet over medium heat. Add 1 quesadilla; cook until cheese starts to melt and bottom is browned, about 2 minutes. Turn over and cook other side until browned. Remove and keep warm while cooking remaining quesadilla. Cut each quesadilla into 8 wedges. Serve with salsa, if desired.   *Makes 2 servings*

## BRUNCH DISHES

## MEDITERRANEAN-STYLE CRAB CAKES

  5 tablespoons butter, divided usage
¼ cup chopped onion
¼ cup chopped celery
  1 clove garlic, minced
  2 cans (6 ounces each) crabmeat, well
    drained
1¼ cups PROGRESSO® Italian Style Bread
    Crumbs, divided usage
¼ cup mayonnaise
  1 egg, lightly beaten
1½ teaspoons Worcestershire sauce
  1 teaspoon freshly squeezed lemon juice
⅛ teaspoon ground black pepper

**1.** In large skillet, heat 1 tablespoon butter. Add onion, celery and garlic; cook 3 minutes or until tender, stirring occasionally.

**2.** Remove skillet from heat. Stir in crabmeat, ¾ cup bread crumbs, mayonnaise, egg, Worcestershire sauce, lemon juice and pepper.

**3.** Shape crabmeat mixture into 4 patties; coat with remaining ½ cup bread crumbs, pressing crumbs onto each patty.

**4.** In same large skillet over medium heat, melt remaining 4 tablespoons butter. Cook patties in butter 8 to 9 minutes or until golden brown on both sides.                   *Makes 4 servings*

**Estimated preparation time:** 15 minutes
**Cooking time:** 8 minutes

## SPINACH CHEESE STRATA

  6 slices whole wheat bread
  2 tablespoons butter or margarine, softened
  1 cup (4 ounces) shredded Cheddar cheese
½ cup (2 ounces) shredded Monterey Jack
    cheese
1¼ cups milk
  6 eggs, lightly beaten
  1 package (10 ounces) frozen spinach,
    thawed and well drained
¼ teaspoon salt
⅛ teaspoon pepper

**1.** Spread bread with butter. Arrange buttered slices in single layer in greased 13×9-inch baking dish. Sprinkle with cheeses.

**2.** Combine milk, eggs, spinach, salt and pepper in large bowl; stir well. Pour over bread and cheese.

**3.** Cover; refrigerate at least 6 hours or overnight.

**4.** Bake, uncovered, at 350°F about 1 hour or until puffy and lightly golden.           *Makes 4 to 6 servings*

## BRUNCH DISHES

## STEAK HASH

2 tablespoons vegetable oil
1 green bell pepper, chopped
½ medium onion, chopped
1 pound russet potatoes, baked, chopped
8 ounces cooked steak or roast beef, cut
    into 1-inch cubes
    Salt and freshly ground pepper
¼ cup (1 ounce) shredded Monterey Jack
    cheese
4 eggs

**1.** Heat oil in medium skillet over medium heat. Add bell pepper and onion; cook until tender. Stir in potatoes; reduce heat to low. Cover and cook, stirring occasionally, about 10 minutes or until potatoes are hot.

**2.** Stir in steak; season with salt and pepper. Sprinkle with cheese. Cover; cook about 5 minutes or until steak is hot and cheese is melted. Spoon onto 4 plates.

**3.** Prepare eggs as desired; top each serving with 1 egg.     *Makes 4 servings*

## LAYERED VEGETABLE BAKE

2 slices day-old white bread, crumbled
2 tablespoons chopped fresh parsley
    (optional)
2 tablespoons butter or margarine, melted
1 large all-purpose potato (about ½ pound),
    thinly sliced
1 large yellow or red bell pepper, sliced
1 envelope LIPTON® Recipe Secrets®
    Savory Herb with Garlic or Golden
    Onion Soup Mix
1 large tomato, sliced

Preheat oven to 375°F.

Spray 1½-quart round casserole or baking dish with no stick cooking spray. In small bowl, combine bread crumbs, parsley and butter; set aside.

In prepared baking dish, arrange potato slices; top with yellow pepper. Sprinkle with savory herb with garlic soup mix. Arrange tomato slices over pepper, overlapping slightly. Sprinkle with bread crumb mixture. Cover with aluminum foil and bake 45 minutes. Remove foil and continue baking 15 minutes or until vegetables are tender.

*Makes about 6 servings*

*Steak Hash*

## BRUNCH DISHES

## WELSH RAREBIT

½ cup HELLMANN'S® or BEST FOODS® Real or Light Mayonnaise or Reduced Fat Cholesterol Free Mayonnaise Dressing
3 tablespoons flour
½ teaspoon dry mustard
½ teaspoon Worcestershire sauce
¾ cup beer
2 cups (8 ounces) shredded Cheddar cheese
8 slices white or whole wheat bread, toasted, halved diagonally
3 large tomatoes, cut into 16 slices

In 2-quart saucepan combine mayonnaise, flour, dry mustard and Worcestershire sauce. Stirring constantly, cook over low heat 1 minute. Gradually stir in beer until thick and smooth (do not boil). Stir in cheese until melted. Arrange 4 toast halves and 4 tomato slices alternately on each of 4 serving plates; spoon on cheese sauce. Serve immediately.

*Makes 4 servings*

**MICROWAVE DIRECTIONS:** In 2-quart microwavable bowl combine mayonnaise, flour, dry mustard and Worcestershire sauce. Gradually stir in beer and cheese. Microwave on HIGH (100%) 4 minutes, stirring vigorously after each minute. Serve as above.

## QUICK APRICOT SYRUP

¾ cup apricot preserves
¾ cup apple juice

Combine preserves and apple juice in medium saucepan over medium heat. Bring to a boil. Cook, stirring occasionally, until slightly thickened. Serve warm over pancakes, waffles or French toast.

*Makes about 1 cup*

> *Try this easy, great-tasting apricot syrup mixed with yogurt or served over hot cereal. Apricots are jam-packed with nutrients that help the body produce vitamin A, which helps to fight the common cold and prevents night blindness.*

*Welsh Rarebit*

## BRUNCH DISHES

## CHICKEN CAESAR SALAD

**1 tablespoon *plus* 1½ teaspoons olive oil**
**4 boneless, skinless chicken breast halves**
**(¾ to 1 pound), cut into strips**
**4 to 5 cups torn romaine lettuce**
**(1 large head)**
**1 large Roma or 1 medium tomato, diced**
**½ cup grated fresh Parmesan cheese**
**1 bottle (8 ounces) LAWRY'S® Creamy**
**Caesar with Cracked Pepper Dressing**
***or* LAWRY'S® Classic Caesar with**
**Imported Anchovies Dressing**
**Seasoned croutons**

In large skillet, heat oil. Add chicken. Sauté 7 to
10 minutes or until no longer pink in center,
stirring frequently. In large salad bowl, combine
lettuce, tomato, Parmesan cheese and chicken; mix
lightly. Refrigerate. Before serving, add enough
dressing to coat all ingredients; toss lightly.
Sprinkle with croutons.       *Makes 4 servings*

**HINT:** For extra flavor, grill chicken breast halves
until no longer pink in center; slice thinly. Serve on
salad.

## MAPLE-GLAZED HAM

**4 slices ham (3 ounces each)**
**¼ cup maple syrup**
**1 teaspoon Dijon-style mustard**

**1.** Preheat broiler.

**2.** Place ham slices on broiler pan. Combine syrup
and mustard in small bowl. Brush each slice with
about 1½ teaspoons of syrup mixture.

**3.** Broil 4 inches below heat about 4 minutes or
until ham starts to brown. Turn and brush with
remaining syrup mixture. Broil until browned.

*Makes 4 servings*

*Chicken Caesar Salad*

## BRUNCH DISHES

## SMOKED SALMON LAVASH

**4 ounces cream cheese, softened**
**1 tablespoon lemon juice**
**¼ teaspoon prepared horseradish**
**4 small (about 5 inches) lavash**
**4 ounces sliced smoked salmon**
**½ red onion, thinly sliced**
**2 tablespoons capers, drained**

Combine cream cheese, lemon juice and horseradish in small bowl. Spread carefully over lavash. Top with salmon, onion and capers.

*Makes 4 servings*

## HASH-AND-EGG BRUNCH

**1 can (12 ounces) corned beef, cut into chunks**
**3 cups frozen hash brown potatoes, thawed**
**1 can (10¾ ounces) condensed cream of celery soup**
**1 can (2.8 ounces) FRENCH'S® French Fried Onions**
**¼ teaspoon pepper**
**6 eggs**
**½ cup (2 ounces) shredded Cheddar cheese**

Preheat oven to 400°. In large bowl, combine corned beef, potatoes, soup, *½ can* French Fried Onions and the pepper. Spoon evenly into 8×12-inch baking dish. Bake, covered, at 400° for 20 minutes or until heated through. Using back of spoon, make 6 wells in hash mixture. Break 1 egg into each well. Bake, uncovered, 15 to 20 minutes or until eggs are cooked to desired doneness. Sprinkle cheese down center of dish and top with remaining onions. Bake, uncovered, 1 to 3 minutes or until onions are golden brown.

*Makes 6 servings*

**MICROWAVE DIRECTIONS:** Prepare corned beef mixture as above; spoon into 8×12-inch microwave-safe dish. Do not add eggs. Cook, uncovered, on HIGH 10 minutes. Rotate dish halfway through cooking time. Place eggs in hash as above. Using a toothpick, pierce each egg yolk and white twice. Cook, covered, 5 to 6 minutes or until eggs are cooked to desired doneness. Rotate dish halfway through cooking time. Top with cheese and remaining onions; cook, uncovered, 1 minute or until cheese melts. Let stand 5 minutes.

*Smoked Salmon Lavash*

## BRUNCH DISHES

## SHRIMP-SPINACH CRÊPE STACK

**1 recipe Creamed Spinach (page 51)**
**1 tablespoon vegetable oil**
**½ medium onion, chopped**
**1 clove garlic, minced**
**8 ounces fresh mushrooms, sliced**
**8 ounces small cooked shrimp**
**2 tablespoons lemon juice**
**¼ teaspoon dried tarragon leaves**
**½ teaspoon salt**
**⅛ teaspoon freshly ground pepper**
**6 (6½-inch) Crêpes (page 24)**
**1 cup (4 ounces) shredded Swiss cheese**

1. Prepare Creamed Spinach; set aside.

2. Heat oil in medium skillet over medium heat; add onion and garlic. Cook, stirring occasionally, until onion is tender. Add mushrooms; cook until mushrooms are tender.

3. Continue cooking until moisture has evaporated. Stir in Creamed Spinach, shrimp, lemon juice, tarragon, salt and pepper.

4. Preheat oven to 375°F. Place 1 crêpe in lightly greased shallow baking dish. Spread ¾ cup shrimp filling over crêpe. Repeat layers with remaining crêpes and filling, ending with crêpe. Sprinkle top with cheese. Bake about 30 minutes or until filling is heated through. Cut into wedges to serve.

*Makes 4 servings*

**ROLLED SHRIMP-SPINACH CRÊPES:** Use 8 (6½-inch) crêpes. Prepare filling as above. Spoon about ⅓ cup of filling on each crêpe. Roll to enclose filling. Place in lightly greased 13×9-inch baking dish. Repeat with remaining crêpes and filling. Sprinkle with cheese. Bake about 15 minutes or until filling is heated through.

*Makes 4 servings*

## PAPAYA-KIWIFRUIT SALAD WITH ORANGE DRESSING

**1 papaya**
**4 kiwifruit**
**6 tablespoons frozen orange juice concentrate, thawed**
**3 tablespoons honey**
**1 cup sour cream**
**1 tablespoon grated orange peel**
**1 tablespoon grated lime peel**

1. Peel and remove seeds from papaya. Slice lengthwise into thin slices.

2. Peel kiwifruit and cut crosswise into thin slices. Arrange papaya and kiwifruit on 4 salad plates.

3. Combine orange juice concentrate and honey in small bowl. Stir in sour cream. Spoon dressing over salads; sprinkle with peels. *Makes 4 servings*

*Top to bottom: Orange Juice & Champagne (page 122) and Shrimp-Spinach Crêpe Stack*

## BRUNCH DISHES

## BLACK BEAN GARNACHAS

**1 can (14½ ounces) DEL MONTE® Mexican
   Style Stewed Tomatoes**
**1 can (15 ounces) black or pinto beans,
   drained**
**2 cloves garlic, minced**
**1 to 2 teaspoons minced jalapeño chiles
   (optional)**
**½ teaspoon ground cumin**
**1 cup cubed grilled chicken**
**4 flour tortillas**
**½ cup shredded sharp Cheddar cheese
   Shredded lettuce and diced avocado
   (optional)**

Drain tomatoes, reserving liquid; chop tomatoes.
In large skillet, combine tomatoes, reserved liquid,
beans, garlic, jalapeño and cumin. Cook over
medium-high heat, 5 to 7 minutes or until
thickened, stirring occasionally. Season with salt
and pepper, if desired. Add chicken. Arrange
tortillas in a single layer on grill over medium
coals. Spread about ¾ cup chicken mixture over
each tortilla. Top with cheese. Cook about 3
minutes or until bottom of tortilla browns and
cheese melts. Garnish with shredded lettuce and
diced avocado, if desired.          *Makes 4 servings*

**Prep time:** 5 minutes
**Cook time:** 10 minutes

## QUICK PAELLA

**1 tablespoon oil**
**1 pound hot Italian sausage, cut into 1-inch
   pieces**
**2 cloves garlic, minced**
**1 tablespoon cornstarch**
**1 can (13¾ ounces) chicken broth**
**1 package (10 ounces) frozen peas and
   pearl onions, thawed**
**½ pound medium shrimp, cleaned**
**1 can (8 ounces) stewed tomatoes**
**1½ cups MINUTE® Original Rice, uncooked**
**⅛ teaspoon saffron or ground turmeric
   (optional)**

**HEAT** oil in large skillet on medium-high heat.
Add sausage and garlic; cook and stir until sausage
is browned.

**MIX** cornstarch and broth until smooth. Stir into
skillet. Add vegetables, shrimp and tomatoes; cook
and stir until mixture thickens and comes to boil.

**STIR** in rice and saffron; cover. Remove from
heat. Let stand 5 minutes. Stir.

*Makes 6 servings*

**Prep Time:** 10 minutes
**Cooking Time:** 15 minutes

*Black Bean Garnachas*

## BRUNCH DISHES

## CALIFORNIA-STYLE TUNA MELTS

4 slices bread, cut in half, *or* 8 thin slices French bread *or* 4 (8-inch) flour tortillas, cut into halves
¼ cup reduced-calorie mayonnaise or salad dressing
8 thin slices tomato
1 can (9¼ ounces) STARKIST® Tuna, drained and flaked
½ cup chopped red onion
  Alfalfa sprouts
1 cup shredded low-fat Cheddar cheese
½ ripe avocado, peeled, pitted and thinly sliced

**TO MICROWAVE:** Toast bread, if desired. Arrange pieces on flat microwavable plate or tray. Spread with mayonnaise. Place 1 tomato slice on each bread half. Top with tuna, onion and alfalfa sprouts, dividing evenly. Sprinkle cheese over tops. Cover with waxed paper. Microwave on HIGH (100% power) for 2 to 4 minutes, or until sandwiches are heated through and cheese is melted, rotating dish once during cooking. Serve topped with avocado slices. Garnish as desired.

*Makes 8 sandwiches, 4 servings*

## VEGETABLE CALZONE

1 loaf (1 pound) frozen bread dough
1 package (10 ounces) frozen chopped broccoli, thawed and well drained
1 cup (8 ounces) SARGENTO® Light Ricotta Cheese
1 cup (4 ounces) SARGENTO® Classic Supreme® Shredded Mozzarella Cheese
1 clove garlic, minced
¼ teaspoon white pepper
1 egg beaten with 1 tablespoon water
1 jar (16 ounces) spaghetti sauce, heated (optional)
  SARGENTO® Grated Parmesan Cheese (optional)

Thaw bread dough; let rise according to package directions. Combine broccoli, Ricotta and Mozzarella cheeses, garlic and pepper. Punch down bread dough; turn out onto lightly floured surface. Divide into 4 equal pieces. One at a time, roll out each piece into 8-inch circle. Place about ¼ cup cheese mixture on half of circle, leaving 1-inch border. Fold dough over to cover filling, forming semi-circle; press and crimp edges with fork tines to seal. Brush with egg mixture. Place on greased baking sheet; bake at 350°F 30 minutes or until brown and puffed. Transfer to rack; cool 10 minutes. Top with hot spaghetti sauce and Parmesan cheese.

*Makes 4 servings*

*California-Style Tuna Melts*

# BRUNCH DISHES

## MEDITERRANEAN PHYLLO PIE

1 cup sliced fresh mushrooms
¾ cup olive oil or melted butter
1 (26-ounce) jar CLASSICO® Di Napoli
   (Tomato & Basil) Pasta Sauce
2 cups chopped cooked chicken
1 (14-ounce) can artichoke hearts, drained
   and chopped *or* 1 (9-ounce) package
   frozen artichoke hearts, thawed, drained
   and chopped
½ cup sliced pitted ripe olives
1 teaspoon WYLER'S® or STEERO®
   Chicken-Flavor Instant Bouillon
1 (16-ounce) package frozen phyllo pastry
   dough, thawed
¾ cup grated Parmesan or Romano cheese

In large skillet, cook mushrooms in *2 tablespoons* oil until tender. Add pasta sauce, chicken, artichokes, olives and bouillon. Bring to a boil; reduce heat and simmer, uncovered, 20 minutes, stirring occasionally. Preheat oven to 400°F. Meanwhile, place 2 pastry sheets on bottom of greased 15 × 10-inch baking pan, pressing into corners. Brush with oil. Working quickly, repeat with pastry and oil, using 2 sheets pastry at a time until 14 sheets have been used. Sprinkle with *¼ cup* cheese. Spread chicken mixture over pastry; top with *¼ cup* cheese. Repeat layering with remaining pastry sheets and oil until all pastry has been used. Trim edges of pastry even with edges of pan. Top with remaining *¼ cup* cheese. Bake 25 to 30 minutes or until golden. Refrigerate leftovers.

*Makes 8 to 10 servings*

## POTATO AND PORK FRITTATA

12 ounces (about 3 cups) frozen hash brown
   potatoes
1 teaspoon Cajun seasoning
4 egg whites
2 whole eggs
¼ cup 1% low fat milk
1 teaspoon dry mustard
¼ teaspoon coarsely ground black pepper
10 ounces (about 3 cups) frozen stir-fry
   vegetables
¾ cup chopped cooked lean pork
½ cup (2 ounces) shredded reduced fat
   Cheddar cheese

**1.** Preheat oven to 400°F. Spray baking sheet with nonstick cooking spray. Spread potatoes on baking sheet; sprinkle with Cajun seasoning. Bake 15 minutes or until hot. Remove from oven. *Reduce oven temperature to 350°F.*

**2.** Beat egg whites, eggs, milk, mustard and pepper in small bowl. Place vegetables and ⅓ cup water in medium nonstick skillet. Cook over medium heat 5 minutes or until vegetables are crisp-tender; drain.

**3.** Add pork and potatoes to vegetables in skillet; stir lightly. Add egg mixture. Sprinkle with cheese. Cook over medium-low heat 5 minutes. Place skillet in 350°F oven and bake 5 minutes or until egg mixture is set and cheese is melted.

*Makes 4 servings*

*Potato and Pork Frittata*

## BRUNCH DISHES

## ORANGE JUICE & CHAMPAGNE

**6 teaspoons orange-flavored liqueur**
**1 quart orange juice, chilled**
**1 bottle (750ml) champagne, chilled**

Pour 1 teaspoon liqueur into each of 6 wine glasses. Fill each two-thirds full with orange juice. Fill glasses with champagne.     *Makes 6 servings*

## CHILIES RELLENOS CASSEROLE

**3 eggs, separated**
**¾ cup milk**
**¾ cup all-purpose flour**
**½ teaspoon salt**
**1 tablespoon butter or margarine**
**½ cup chopped onion**
**2 cans (7 ounces each) whole green chilies, drained**
**8 slices (1 ounce each) Monterey Jack cheese, cut into halves**
  **Garnishes: Sour cream, sliced green onions, pitted ripe olive slices, guacamole and salsa**

**1.** Preheat oven to 350°F.

**2.** Combine egg yolks, milk, flour and salt in blender or food processor. Cover; process until smooth. Pour into medium bowl and let stand.

**3.** Melt butter in small skillet over medium heat. Add onion; cook until tender.

**4.** Pat chilies dry with paper towels. Slit each chili lengthwise and carefully remove seeds. Place 2 halves of cheese and 1 tablespoon onion in each chili; reshape chilies to cover cheese.

**5.** Place chilies in single layer in greased 13×9-inch baking dish.

**6.** In small clean bowl, beat egg whites until soft peaks form; fold into yolk mixture. Pour over chilies.

**7.** Bake 20 to 25 minutes or until topping is puffed and knife inserted in center comes out clean. Broil 4 inches below heat 30 seconds or until topping is golden brown. Serve with desired garnishes.

*Makes 4 servings*

# *——Acknowledgments——*

**The publisher would like to thank the companies and organizations listed below for the use of their recipes and photos in this publication.**

Best Foods, a Division of CPC International Inc.
Borden Kitchens, Borden, Inc.
The Dannon Company, Inc.
Del Monte Corporation
Kraft Foods, Inc.
Lawry's® Foods, Inc.
Thomas J. Lipton Co.
Oscar Mayer Foods Corporation
Pet Incorporated
Reckitt & Colman Inc.
Riviana Foods Inc.
Sargento Foods Inc.®
StarKist Seafood Company

# MENUS

## Summer Celebration Buffet

Sparkling Apple Punch (page 100)

Ham & Swiss Cheese Biscuits (page 69)

California Croissants (page 54)

Endive-Tomato Salad (page 98)

Roasted Vegetable Omelet with Fresh Salsa
(page 52)

Apple-Almond Coffee Cakes (page 70)

fresh fruit

## Down-Home Country Breakfast

fresh-squeezed orange juice

Three-Egg Omelet (page 6)

Spicy Sausage Skillet Breakfast (page 38)

Garlic Skillet Potatoes (page 10)

Caramel-Topped Mega Muffins (page 72)

Spicy Sweet Potato Muffins (page 78)

coffee

## Hearty Eye-Opener

Steak Hash (page 106)

Sausage Gravy (page 20)

Baking Powder Biscuits (page 16)

milk, juice and coffee

## Springtime Brunch

Sparkling White Sangria (page 88)

Egg Blossoms (page 42)

Waffles (page 8) with Quick Apricot Syrup
(108)

maple-cured bacon

a selection of herbal teas

# MENUS

## Bridal Shower Brunch Buffet

Orange Juice & Champagne (page 122)
Berry Crêpes with Orange Sauce (page 10)
California-Style Tuna Melts (page 118)
Chicken Caesar Salad (page 110)
Apricot Ring (page 76)
Roasted Red Pepper Biscuits (page 72)

## Chocolate Lover's Breakfast

Chocolate Waffles (page 62)
bagels with Chocolate-Cream Bagel Spread
(page 28)
Chocolate Chunk Sour Cream Muffins
(page 84)
Hot Chocolate (page 8)
coffee and milk

## Simple Make-Ahead Brunch

assorted juices
Feta Brunch Bake (page 92)
Lemon Yogurt Coffee Cake (page 82)
toasted bagels with Bagel Toppers (page 28)

## New Year's Day Breakfast

tomato juice
Scrambled Eggs (page 14)
Potato-Carrot Pancakes (page 24)
Maple-Glazed Ham (page 110)
Pecan Sticky Buns (page 80)
Muffin Surprise (page 78)

# —Index—

# METRIC CONVERSION CHART

## VOLUME MEASUREMENTS (dry)

$\frac{1}{8}$ teaspoon = 0.5 mL
$\frac{1}{4}$ teaspoon = 1 mL
$\frac{1}{2}$ teaspoon = 2 mL
$\frac{3}{4}$ teaspoon = 4 mL
1 teaspoon = 5 mL
1 tablespoon = 15 mL
2 tablespoons = 30 mL
$\frac{1}{4}$ cup = 60 mL
$\frac{1}{3}$ cup = 75 mL
$\frac{1}{2}$ cup = 125 mL
$\frac{2}{3}$ cup = 150 mL
$\frac{3}{4}$ cup = 175 mL
1 cup = 250 mL
2 cups = 1 pint = 500 mL
3 cups = 750 mL
4 cups = 1 quart = 1 L

## VOLUME MEASUREMENTS (fluid)

1 fluid ounce (2 tablespoons) = 30 mL
4 fluid ounces ($\frac{1}{2}$ cup) = 125 mL
8 fluid ounces (1 cup) = 250 mL
12 fluid ounces (1$\frac{1}{2}$ cups) = 375 mL
16 fluid ounces (2 cups) = 500 mL

## WEIGHTS (mass)

$\frac{1}{2}$ ounce = 15 g
1 ounce = 30 g
3 ounces = 90 g
4 ounces = 120 g
8 ounces = 225 g
10 ounces = 285 g
12 ounces = 360 g
16 ounces = 1 pound = 450 g

## DIMENSIONS

$\frac{1}{16}$ inch = 2 mm
$\frac{1}{8}$ inch = 3 mm
$\frac{1}{4}$ inch = 6 mm
$\frac{1}{2}$ inch = 1.5 cm
$\frac{3}{4}$ inch = 2 cm
1 inch = 2.5 cm

## OVEN TEMPERATURES

250°F = 120°C
275°F = 140°C
300°F = 150°C
325°F = 160°C
350°F = 180°C
375°F = 190°C
400°F = 200°C
425°F = 220°C
450°F = 230°C

## BAKING PAN SIZES

| Utensil | Size in Inches/Quarts | Metric Volume | Size in Centimeters |
|---|---|---|---|
| Baking or Cake Pan (square or rectangular) | 8×8×2 | 2 L | 20×20×5 |
| | 9×9×2 | 2.5 L | 22×22×5 |
| | 12×8×2 | 3 L | 30×20×5 |
| | 13×9×2 | 3.5 L | 33×23×5 |
| Loaf Pan | 8×4×3 | 1.5 L | 20×10×7 |
| | 9×5×3 | 2 L | 23×13×7 |
| Round Layer Cake Pan | 8×1½ | 1.2 L | 20×4 |
| | 9×1½ | 1.5 L | 23×4 |
| Pie Plate | 8×1¼ | 750 mL | 20×3 |
| | 9×1¼ | 1 L | 23×3 |
| Baking Dish or Casserole | 1 quart | 1 L | — |
| | 1½ quart | 1.5 L | — |
| | 2 quart | 2 L | — |